bowls

13-Digit ISBN: 978-1-40034-643-1
10-Digit ISBN: 1-40034-643-6

Cider Mill Press Book Publishers
"Where good books are ready for press"
501 Nelson Place
Nashville, Tennessee 37214

cidermillpress.com

Typography: Neulis Sans

Image Credits: All photos courtesy of Ayesha Singh.

Printed in Canada
24 25 26 27 28 TC 5 4 3 2 1

First Edition

bowls

100+ recipes for healthy, vibrant bowls

AYESHA SINGH

CIDER MILL PRESS

BOOK PUBLISHERS

contents

introduction

Welcome to my kitchen, a place where flavors converge, cultures mingle, and meals are served with a generous helping of love. As I invite you to join my culinary journey, I am filled with gratitude for where it has led so far—from the bustling streets of India to the vibrant neighborhoods of America.

This is my little piece of the culinary world, where every meal is an adventure, and every bite is a celebration of flavors from around the globe. Join me as we embark on this adventure that traverses India, the United States, and everywhere in between, weaving together the rich tapestry of traditions and innovations that define my culinary identity.

I grew up in a household brimming with aromatic spices and bustling with the laughter of family gatherings, and my earliest memories are filled with the sights, sounds, and aromas of my parents' kitchen. Between my mom, who is a passionate cook, and a younger brother who was always eager to lend a hand, our kitchen was a melting pot of perspectives and palates. My family valued food as a means of both sustenance and celebration, and it seemed that our home was always buzzing with activity, from the sizzle of spices in the pan to the laughter of relatives gathered around the table. It was here, amidst the warmth and chaos of family gatherings, that I first fell in love with the art of cooking.

I learned the fundamentals of Indian cuisine from my mom, whose passion for cooking was matched only by her love for her family. Together, we would spend hours in the kitchen, kneading dough for homemade roti, grinding spices for aromatic curries, and experimenting with recipes that had been passed down through generations. From festive feasts to simple weekday meals, our kitchen was a sanctuary—a place where we could come together, share stories, and nourish our bodies and souls.

Leaving home after high school to attend college in a faraway Indian state marked a significant turning point in my culinary journey. Suddenly, I found myself hundreds of miles away from the familiar comforts of my parents' kitchen, thrust into a world where meal prep fell squarely on my shoulders. As a teenager navigating the challenges of college life, I quickly realized the value of the delicious food that had always been readily available at home. On campus, where schedules were packed and resources were limited, finding time and money for nourishing meals became a major challenge.

Yet, amidst the demands of college life, I discovered a newfound appreciation for the culinary skills instilled in me by my parents. With each meal I prepared for myself and my friends, I found solace in the act of cooking—a tangible connection to the warmth and comfort of home. The teenager in me began to understand the depth of my parents' efforts, love, and sacrifices, and I felt a growing sense of gratitude for all that they had provided. Cooking became not just a means of sustenance, but a form of self-expression—a way to honor my heritage and share the flavors of home with those around me.

As I experimented with new recipes and techniques, I received enthusiastic feedback from friends, who marveled at the flavors and aromas emanating from my humble kitchen. Their encouragement and appreciation further fueled my passion for cooking, inspiring me to dig deeper into the world of culinary arts.

After graduating from college, I embarked on a new chapter of my life, starting with my first job in the bustling metropolis of Delhi. Surrounded by the sights, sounds, and flavors of the vibrant city, I continued to hone my culinary skills, drawing inspiration from the rich tapestry of Indian cuisine that surrounded me.

Just about a year later, after tying the knot and beginning a new chapter of my life in the United States, my culinary journey reached new heights.

Settling in the heart of the Big Apple—New York City—marked a significant milestone in my evolution as a cook. Here, amidst the towering skyscrapers and bustling streets, I found myself immersed in a melting pot of cultures and cuisines, each offering its own unique flavors and traditions. With each bite of street food and each visit to a new restaurant, my fascination with food grew deeper, and my desire to explore the world's cuisines became impossible to ignore.

Throughout this journey, I received unwavering support and encouragement from my husband, whose love for food mirrored my own. Together, we embarked on many adventures, exploring new neighborhoods, trying new dishes, and experimenting with new ingredients. He has been a constant source of inspiration, spurring me on to new heights in the kitchen and beyond.

As life carried us from one American coast to the other, it was in California, with its golden shores and bountiful produce, that I found a new canvas for my culinary experiments. Inspired by the abundance of fresh ingredients and the spirit of innovation that permeates the West Coast, I began to explore flavors from across the globe. From Indian-inspired tacos to masala-tinged burgers, each dish became a testament to the rich tapestry of cultures that defines contemporary American cuisine.

Now, nestled in the verdant landscapes of the greater Washington D.C. area, I find myself at the intersection of tradition and modernity, nostalgia and novelty. Here, amidst the cherry blossoms and historic landmarks, I draw inspiration from the vibrant community of food lovers who share my passion for culinary exploration. Making a life here with my husband and our lively 5-year-old son, our kitchen has taken its rightful place at the heart of our home—a place where we come together to share meals, stories, and laughter. Our kitchen is more than just a place to cook—it's a playground of possibilities and a sanctuary of love. Drawing on my Indian heritage and the diverse culinary influences of my adopted home, I create food that nourishes the body, delights the senses, and brings joy to the soul. Whether it's a comforting bowl of dal served with fragrant basmati rice, a vibrant salad bursting with seasonal vegetables, or a decadent dessert that satisfies the inevitable sweet cravings, each dish is a celebration of flavors, textures, and traditions.

In *Bowls*, I invite you to join me on my latest culinary adventure, one that celebrates the joy of cooking, the beauty of simplicity, and the endless possibilities of flavor. From hearty breakfast bowls to satisfying dinners, each recipe is crafted with care and infused with the spirit of gratitude, joy, inspiration, and playfulness that permeates my own kitchen.

Whether you're a seasoned home cook or a novice in the kitchen, there is something here for everyone—a recipe to inspire, a dish to delight, and a blissful bowl waiting to be savored. As you embark on this culinary journey with me, I encourage you to approach each recipe with an open heart and a playful spirit. Experiment with flavors, textures, and ingredients, and don't be afraid to make each preparation your own. And above all, remember to savor every moment—the laughter of loved ones gathered around the table, the aroma of spices wafting from the stove, and the simple joy of sharing a meal with those you hold dear.

breakfast

Most people's focus in the morning is simply getting out the door and getting to work on time. These recipes allow you to retain that focus, while also ensuring that you have enough fuel to get you through the day.

yield: 1 serving / active time: 15 minutes / total time: 15 minutes

the ultimate oatmeal

Comforting, nourishing, and heart-warming, a warm bowl of oatmeal is almost akin to a warm hug from mom—the key word being almost. This bowl is super easy to scale up to provide more servings, and also requires very little effort to tailor to your or another loved one's taste.

1 cup water

½ cup old-fashioned oats

Pinch of kosher salt

¼ teaspoon cinnamon

¼ cup milk

Chunky Monkey (optional; see page 245)

Berry Blast (optional; see page 245)

Cinnamon Apple (optional; see page 246)

1 Place the water in a small saucepan and warm it over medium heat. Stir in the oats, salt, and cinnamon and bring to a gentle boil.

2 Reduce the heat to low, add the milk, and cook until the oats are tender and creamy, about 6 minutes, stirring occasionally.

3 Transfer the oatmeal to a bowl, top it with Chunky Monkey, Berry Blast, Cinnamon Apple, or any of your preferred accompaniments, and serve.

yogurt & granola

Once you have made granola at home, you're never going back to a store-bought version.

5 tablespoons unsalted butter

¾ cup brown sugar

1 tablespoon maple syrup

1 tablespoon pure vanilla extract

Pinch of kosher salt

2 cups old-fashioned oats

1 cup chopped almonds

¾ cup chopped cashews

½ cup coconut flakes

1 teaspoon cinnamon

1 cup dark chocolate chips

½ cup raisins

⅓ cup pumpkin seeds

2 cups Greek yogurt

1 cup raspberries

1   Preheat the oven to 300°F and line a baking sheet with parchment paper. Place the butter in a medium saucepan and melt it over low heat. Add the brown sugar and maple syrup and cook, stirring occasionally, until the sugar has dissolved. Stir in the vanilla and salt and remove the pan from heat.

2   Place the oats, almonds, cashews, coconut flakes, and cinnamon in a large mixing bowl, pour the melted butter mixture over the oat mixture, and stir until everything is well combined.

3   Spread the granola in an even layer on the baking sheet. Place the granola in the oven and bake until it is golden brown and crunchy, about 30 minutes, rotating the pan and stirring the granola halfway through.

4   Remove the granola from the oven and let it cool completely.

5   Stir the chocolate chips, raisins, and pumpkin seeds into the granola. You can store this granola in an airtight container for up to 2 weeks.

6   Divide the yogurt among the serving bowls, top each portion with some of the granola and raspberries, and serve.

yield: 2 to 4 servings / active time: 25 minutes / total time: 25 minutes

tex-mex breakfast

Take these delicious, easy-to-put-together bowls as a sign that it's time to host a Sunday brunch at home.

3 strips of bacon

6 to 8 eggs

2 cups spring mix

Pico de Gallo (see page 246)

Flesh of 2 large avocados, sliced

½ cup shredded cheddar cheese

¼ cup chopped fresh cilantro

6 small flour tortillas, warmed, for serving

1   Place the bacon in a large skillet and cook it over medium heat until it is crispy, about 8 minutes, turning it as necessary. Transfer the bacon to a paper towel–lined plate to drain and cool. When it is cool enough to handle, chop the bacon and set it aside.

2   Add the eggs to the skillet and fry them until the whites are set and the yolks are cooked to your liking.

3   Divide the spring mix among the serving bowls, top each portion with 2 eggs and some of the Pico de Gallo, avocado, bacon, cheddar cheese, and cilantro, and serve with the tortillas.

see page 15

yield: 1 serving / active time: 5 minutes / total time: 2 hours and 5 minutes

chia pudding

The first time I tried chia pudding was over a decade ago, at a breakfast event in Manhattan, and I've been making them regularly since. What I love is how easy it is to switch up the toppings and keep things fresh.

2 tablespoons chia seeds

1 teaspoon maple syrup

½ cup soy milk (or preferred milk)

1 tablespoon vanilla protein powder (optional)

Granola, for topping (optional)

Peanut butter, for topping (optional)

Strawberries, for topping (optional)

Raspberries, for topping (optional)

1 Place the chia seeds, syrup, and soy milk in a jar and stir until well combined. Let the mixture settle for 1 to 2 minutes and then stir again until the mixture has no clumps.

2 Cover the jar and store it in the refrigerator for at least 2 hours.

3 If you want to add more protein, add the protein powder to the pudding and stir until it is incorporated.

4 Place the pudding in a bowl, top it with granola, peanut butter, or berries (if desired), and serve.

yield: 2 to 4 servings / active time: 20 minutes / total time: 30 minutes

power up bowls

These bowls will have you and your family ready for anything life throws at ya!

2 tablespoons extra-virgin olive oil

1 lb. chicken sausage, chopped

3 cups peeled and diced yellow potatoes

1 white onion, chopped

½ teaspoon garlic powder

½ teaspoon kosher salt

½ teaspoon black pepper

1 teaspoon red pepper flakes

2 to 4 eggs

2 cups baby spinach or spring mix

Flesh of 1 large avocado, sliced

Hemp seeds, for garnish

Sesame seeds, for garnish

Hot sauce, for serving

1 Place half of the olive oil in a large skillet and warm it over medium heat. Add the chicken sausage and cook, stirring occasionally, until it is browned all over, 6 to 8 minutes. Remove the sausage from the pan and set it aside.

2 Add the potatoes to the skillet and cook until they start to brown, 6 to 8 minutes, stirring frequently. Stir in the onion, garlic powder, salt, pepper, and red pepper flakes and cook until the potatoes are tender, 10 to 12 minutes.

3 While the potatoes are cooking, place the remaining olive oil in a separate pan and warm it over medium heat. Add the eggs and cook until the whites are set and the yolks are to your liking.

4 Divide the spinach among the serving bowls and top each portion with some of the potatoes, sausage, and avocado, and a fried egg. Garnish with hemp seeds and sesame seeds and serve with hot sauce.

yield: 4 servings / active time: 10 minutes / total time: 30 minutes

breakfast on the go

Considered the most important meal of the day by the old adage, breakfast is essential but does not have to be complicated. The key to an awesome day is a protein rich breakfast. When I'm expecting a busy week, I pack this version on the go.

8 eggs

Flesh of 2 avocados

6 to 8 black olives, pitted

4 oz. feta cheese, crumbled

1 tablespoon extra-virgin olive oil

½ teaspoon kosher salt

1 teaspoon black pepper

1 teaspoon red pepper flakes

1   Prepare an ice bath. Place the eggs in a large pot and cover them with cold water by 1 inch. Bring the water to a boil. As soon as the water starts to boil, turn off the heat, and cover the pot. Let the eggs sit in the hot water for 10 minutes. Transfer the eggs to the ice bath and let them sit for 12 minutes.

2   Peel the eggs and divide them, the avocados, olives, and feta among the serving bowls.

3   Drizzle the olive oil over each portion, season with the salt, pepper, and red pepper flakes, and serve.

yield: 2 servings / active time: 20 minutes / total time: 30 minutes

acai bowls

These bowls are my go-to for breakfast, and dinner after an exceptionally busy day, as this nutrient-dense, naturally sweet superfood lets you get creative with toppings.

2 (14 oz.) packets of unsweetened frozen acai berry blend

2 peeled bananas, frozen

½ cup nondairy milk

2 tablespoons hemp seeds

2 tablespoons peanut butter

6 to 8 strawberries, hulled and sliced

¼ cup blackberries

½ cup granola

Dark chocolate, shaved, for garnish

1 Place the acai berry blend, bananas, and half of the milk in a food processor and blitz until combined.

2 Wait 30 seconds, add the remaining milk, and blitz until smooth.

3 Divide the puree among the serving bowls and top each portion with some of the hemp seeds, peanut butter, berries, and granola. Garnish with dark chocolate shavings and serve.

yield: 2 to 4 servings / active time: 15 minutes / total time: 15 minutes

turkish eggs

The first time I tried this dish was when I lived in New York City and it was recommended by the owner of the restaurant. In short, I was blown away by the flavors! My favorite version is to enjoy it with some crusty bread and wipe up every last tasty bit.

2 cups Greek yogurt

½ teaspoon kosher salt

2 tablespoons extra-virgin olive oil

6 to 8 eggs

Parsley & Chili Oil (see page 234), warm

Fresh herbs, for garnish

Za'atar, for garnish

Crusty bread, for serving (optional)

1 Place the yogurt and salt in a bowl and stir to combine. Spread the yogurt over the serving plates; you want it to be about 1 inch thick.

2 Place the olive oil in a large skillet and warm it over medium-high heat. Working in batches to avoid crowding the pan, add the eggs and cook until the whites are set and the yolks are to your liking.

3 Place the eggs on top of the yogurt and drizzle the chili oil over each portion. Garnish with herbs and za'atar and serve with crusty bread (if desired).

yield: 1 serving / active time: 10 minutes / total time: 24 hours

overnight oats

I always loved the texture and taste of overnight oats, but wanted more protein for breakfast. This simple twist accomplishes just that.

½ cup rolled oats

½ cup milk

1 tablespoon chia seeds

1 tablespoon vanilla protein powder

½ teaspoon cinnamon

1 teaspoon peanut butter

Honey, to taste

Berries, for garnish

Dark chocolate, chopped, for garnish (optional)

1   Place the oats, milk, chia seeds, protein powder, cinnamon, peanut butter, and honey in a mason jar and stir until combined.

2   Cover the jar tightly and chill it in the refrigerator overnight.

3   The next morning, garnish the oats with berries and chocolate (if desired) and serve.

yield: 2 to 4 servings / active time: 20 minutes / total time: 30 minutes

shakshuka

For a bowl that looks awesome but is rather easy to put together, look no further than a Shakshuka. This one-pan breakfast with poached eggs, simmered in an incredibly flavorful tomato sauce, Shakshuka is popular in many parts of North Africa and the Middle East. Try with sourdough bread, pita, or by itself!

2 tablespoons extra-virgin olive oil

1 garlic clove, minced

1 onion, diced

1 red bell pepper, stemmed, seeded, and chopped

1 teaspoon paprika

½ teaspoon cumin

2 cups Arrabbiata Sauce (see page 228)

Salt, to taste

6 to 8 large eggs

1 bunch of fresh cilantro, chopped, for garnish

1 bunch of fresh parsley, chopped, for garnish

1 cup crumbled feta cheese, for garnish

1   Place the olive oil in a large, deep skillet and warm it over medium heat. Add the garlic and cook for 1 minute.

2   Add the onion and bell pepper and cook, stirring frequently, until they have softened, about 5 minutes.

3   Add the paprika, cumin, and sauce, season with salt, and simmer for 5 minutes.

4   Using a large wooden spoon, make small wells in the sauce and crack 1 egg into each well. Cook until the whites are set and the yolks are to your liking.

5   Divide the shakshuka among the serving bowls, garnish with the cilantro, parsley, and feta, and serve.

from the garden:
salads & plant-based bowls

We all know that we need to incorporate more vegetables into our diet, but putting that into practice is another matter. These dynamic salads and vegetarian bowls make that hurdle effortless to clear, and ensure that your diet is always in balance.

vegan poke

The first time I tried a poke bowl we were living in California and it was the food of the moment. At the time, if I'm being completely honest, I wasn't a fan. However, a few months later I discovered a vegan poke bowl and was blown away by the textures and flavors. I hope this one brings you the same kind of joy.

1 cup sushi rice

2 tablespoons rice vinegar

14 oz. extra-firm tofu, drained

1 tablespoon canola oil

¼ cup soy sauce

2 tablespoons sriracha

1 tablespoon toasted sesame oil

1 large carrot, peeled and grated

6 scallions, trimmed and chopped on a bias

Flesh of 1 large avocado, sliced

⅓ cup shredded cabbage

2 sheets of seaweed

Roasted peanuts, crushed, for garnish

Sesame seeds, for garnish

1 Cook the rice according to the directions on the package. Stir in the vinegar and set the rice aside.

2 Pat the tofu dry with paper towels and dice it. Place the canola oil in a large skillet and warm it over medium heat. Add the tofu and cook until it is browned all over, about 8 minutes, stirring occasionally.

3 Place the soy sauce, sriracha, and sesame oil in a bowl and stir to combine. Pour the sauce over the tofu and stir to combine. Remove the pan from heat.

4 Divide the rice among the bowls and top each portion with some of the carrot, scallions, avocado, cabbage, seaweed, and tofu. Garnish with peanuts and sesame seeds and serve.

yield: 4 servings / active time: 25 minutes / total time: 45 minutes

chana masala

Chana masala, a popular dish from North Indian cuisine, is one of the best ways to level up chickpeas.

2 tablespoons avocado oil

1 large onion, finely diced

Salt, to taste

½ teaspoon cumin

1 teaspoon coriander

4 garlic cloves, minced

1-inch piece of ginger, peeled and minced

1 teaspoon Kashmiri chili powder

½ teaspoon turmeric

½ teaspoon garam masala

1 (28 oz.) can of tomato puree

2 (14 oz.) cans of chickpeas, drained

1 cup water

Fresh cilantro or mint, chopped, for garnish

Naan, for serving

Pickled Vegetables (see page 240), for serving

1 Place the avocado oil in a saucepan and warm it over medium heat. Add the onion and cook, stirring occasionally, until it starts to brown, 6 to 8 minutes.

2 Season with salt, add the cumin, coriander, garlic, ginger, chili powder, turmeric, and garam masala, and cook for 1 minute.

3 Add the tomato puree and cook until the fat separates from the sauce.

4 Stir in the chickpeas and water and cook until the chickpeas have softened and the dish thickens slightly, about 8 minutes.

5 Ladle the dish into the serving bowls, garnish with cilantro, and serve with Naan and Pickled Vegetables.

yield: 4 servings / active time: 15 minutes / total time: 45 minutes

quinoa & chickpeas, mediterranean style

A protein-packed vegetarian option that is also high in fiber, this bowl will keep you satisfied and has a low glycemic index, which is great for your overall well-being. It is no wonder the Mediterranean diet tops the charts in so many studies based around wellness. Add a dash of flavor and we're off to the races!

1 tablespoon extra-virgin olive oil

1 teaspoon garlic powder

1 teaspoon turmeric

1 teaspoon paprika

1 teaspoon red pepper flakes

½ teaspoon cumin

½ teaspoon kosher salt

1 (14 oz.) can of chickpeas, drained and rinsed

2 cups quinoa

2 cups baby spinach

⅓ cup Pickled Red Onion (see page 228)

⅓ cup chopped Persian cucumbers

⅓ cup Tzatziki (see page 249)

2 tablespoons Harissa Sauce (see page 229)

Feta cheese, crumbled, for garnish

1 Preheat the oven to 375°F. Place the olive oil, garlic powder, turmeric, paprika, red pepper flakes, cumin, and salt in a mixing bowl and stir to combine. Add the chickpeas, stir to coat, and place them on a baking sheet in an even layer.

2 Place the chickpeas in the oven and bake until they are crunchy and golden brown, about 35 minutes.

3 While the chickpeas are in the oven, cook the quinoa according to the directions on the package. Fluff it with a fork and set it aside.

4 Remove the chickpeas from the oven. Divide the quinoa among the serving bowls and top each portion with some of the chickpeas, spinach, pickled onion, cucumber, Tzatziki, and harissa. Garnish with feta and serve.

For the Bowls

2 tablespoons extra-virgin olive oil

1 teaspoon kosher salt

½ teaspoon turmeric

½ teaspoon cinnamon

3 garlic cloves, minced

½ teaspoon cumin

1 teaspoon cayenne pepper

1 large head of cauliflower, trimmed and cut into small florets

1 red onion, sliced thin

3 cups chopped lettuce

2 Persian cucumbers, sliced thin

Fresh parsley, for garnish

Fresh mint, for garnish

Pickled radishes, sliced thin, for garnish

Pickled Red Onion (see page 228), for garnish

Flour tortillas, for serving

Sriracha, for garnish

For the Sauce

¼ cup Greek yogurt

2 tablespoons mayonnaise

1 garlic clove, grated

1 teaspoon extra-virgin olive oil

¼ teaspoon kosher salt

cauliflower shawarma

Cauliflower's recent renaissance is due in large part to its ability to take on a wide range of flavors, a talent showcased beautifully in this dynamic bowl.

1 Preheat the oven to 425°F. To begin preparations for the bowls, place the olive oil, salt, turmeric, cinnamon, garlic, cumin, and cayenne in a bowl and stir to combine. Add the cauliflower and toss to coat. Place the cauliflower in an even layer on half of a baking sheet and place the fresh red onion in an even layer on the other half. Place the vegetables in the oven and roast until they are tender and golden brown, about 25 minutes, turning them over halfway through.

2 While the vegetables are roasting in the oven, prepare the sauce. Place all of the ingredients in a mixing bowl and stir to combine. Set the sauce aside.

3 Remove the vegetables from the oven. Divide the lettuce among the serving bowls and top with the roasted cauliflower and onion, and the cucumber. Drizzle the sauce over each portion, garnish with parsley, mint, radishes, pickled onion, and sriracha, and serve.

yield: 4 servings / active time: 15 minutes / total time: 25 minutes

spicy tofu

Chili paneer is an Indo-Chinese dish that is believed to have originated in East India—arguably, of course. Even though no one is quite certain of the origins, it has found its way to tables all across the globe, and is the inspiration for this tofu-centered version.

1 cup rice

14 oz. extra-firm tofu, drained

2 tablespoons cornstarch

Salt, to taste

3 tablespoons avocado oil

¼ cup sriracha

1 tablespoon white vinegar

2 tablespoons ketchup

2 garlic cloves, minced

¼ cup soy sauce

1 large red onion, diced

1 large bell pepper, stemmed, seeded, and diced

Scallions, chopped on a bias, for garnish

1 Cook the rice according to the directions on the package. Fluff it, cover it, and set the rice aside.

2 Pat the tofu dry and cut it into cubes. Place the cornstarch and salt in a shallow bowl, add the tofu, and toss to coat.

3 Place 1 tablespoon of avocado oil in a large skillet and warm it over medium heat. Add the tofu and cook until it is well browned, about 8 minutes.

4 Place the sriracha, vinegar, ketchup, garlic, soy sauce, and remaining avocado oil in a bowl and whisk to combine. Add the sauce to the skillet along with the onion and pepper and gently stir to combine.

5 Cook for 2 to 3 minutes, until the sauce is warmed through.

6 Divide the rice among the serving bowls and top each portion with some of the tofu mixture.

7 Garnish with scallions and serve.

yield: 4 servings / active time: 10 minutes / total time: 30 minutes

thai quinoa salad

This simple, crunchy salad features a creamy peanut butter dressing that is kind of addictive. It's also a great make-ahead dinner, as it tastes even better the next day.

For the Dressing

⅓ cup creamy peanut butter

1 tablespoon soy sauce

1½ tablespoons sriracha

1 teaspoon maple syrup

2 tablespoons water

1 teaspoon kosher salt

Juice of 1 lime

For the Bowls

1 cup quinoa

2 cups chopped cucumbers

1 red bell pepper, stemmed, seeded, and chopped

2 cups shelled, cooked edamame

¼ cup chopped scallions

1 cup diced carrot

⅓ cup crushed roasted peanuts, for garnish

Fresh cilantro, chopped, for garnish

Lime wedges, for serving

1 To prepare the dressing, place all of the ingredients in a bowl and whisk until well combined. Set the dressing aside.

2 Cook the quinoa according to the directions on the package. Fluff it and transfer it to a mixing bowl. Add cucumbers, pepper, edamame, scallions, and carrot and toss to combine.

3 Add the dressing and toss to combine. Divide the salad among the serving bowls, garnish with peanuts and cilantro, and serve with lime wedges.

yield: 4 servings / active time: 20 minutes / total time: 30 minutes

comforting curry noodles

These warming bowls make for a great weeknight meal on those days when you or a loved one needs a little extra comfort.

½ lb. rice or egg noodles

2 tablespoons avocado oil

3 garlic cloves, chopped

1 red onion, chopped

1 tablespoon minced fresh ginger

½ teaspoon turmeric

½ teaspoon cumin

1 teaspoon red pepper flakes

1 teaspoon kosher salt

1 bell pepper, stemmed, seeded, and diced

2 cups frozen shelled edamame, thawed

2 carrots, chopped

½ cup water

1 (14 oz.) can of coconut milk

Juice of 1 lime

½ teaspoon sugar

Scallions, chopped, for garnish

Chili Oil (see page 247), for garnish

1 Cook the noodles according to the directions on the package. Drain the noodles and set them aside.

2 Place the avocado oil in a large saucepan or Dutch oven and warm it over medium heat. Add the garlic, onion, and ginger and cook, stirring occasionally, until the onion is translucent, about 3 minutes.

3 Stir in the turmeric, cumin, red pepper flakes, and salt. Add the pepper, edamame, and carrots and cook, stirring occasionally, until they start to soften, about 5 minutes.

4 Add the coconut milk and water to the pot and bring to a simmer. Cook, stirring occasionally, until the curry thickens slightly and flavors have developed to your liking.

5 Add the noodles, lime juice, and sugar and toss to combine.

6 Divide the noodles among the serving bowls, garnish with scallions and Chili Oil, and serve.

tofu makhani

Every bit of this North Indian dish is indulgent, featuring an incredible savory depth. If you'd like to make this vegan, substitute cashew cream for the heavy cream.

⅔ cup rice

2 tablespoons avocado oil

14 oz. firm tofu, drained

1 yellow onion, chopped

4 garlic cloves, minced

1 green chile pepper, stemmed, seeded, and diced

3 tablespoons tomato paste

1 teaspoon cumin

1 teaspoon coriander

1 teaspoon kosher salt

1 teaspoon garam masala

1 teaspoon cayenne pepper

½ cup water

¼ cup heavy cream

2 cups chopped lettuce

2 Persian cucumbers, chopped

Pickled Red Onion (see page 228)

Cilantro Chutney (see page 242)

½ teaspoon dried fenugreek, for garnish

Fresh cilantro, chopped, for garnish

1   Cook the rice according to the directions on the package. Fluff it, cover it, and set the rice aside.

2   Place 1 tablespoon of avocado oil in a large skillet and warm it over medium heat. Pat the tofu dry and cook until it is browned all over, about 8 minutes, turning it as necessary. Remove the tofu from the pan and let it cool. When it is cool enough to handle, cut the tofu into cubes.

3   Add the remaining avocado oil to the skillet and warm it over medium heat. Add the yellow onion and cook, stirring occasionally, until it starts to brown, 6 to 8 minutes. Add the garlic and chile and cook, stirring frequently, for 2 minutes.

4   Stir in the tomato paste, cumin, coriander, salt, garam masala, and cayenne and cook for 4 minutes. Add the water, raise the heat to medium-high, and cook, stirring continually, until the sauce thickens slightly.

5   Stir in the cream, add the tofu, and cook until everything is warmed through, about 2 minutes.

6   Divide the rice among the serving bowls and top each portion with some of the tofu mixture, lettuce, cucumbers, pickled onion, and chutney. Garnish with the fenugreek and cilantro and serve.

tofu makhani,
see page 47

yield: 4 servings / active time: 30 minutes / total time: 45 minutes

black bean tofu

A great dish for folks who want to eat healthy but still want boldly flavored meals.

½ cup jasmine rice

14 oz. extra-firm tofu, drained

1 tablespoon cornstarch

Salt, to taste

2 tablespoons coconut oil

1 large onion, diced

1 large bell pepper, stemmed, seeded, and diced

2 dried red chile peppers, stemmed, seeded, and chopped

8 small broccoli florets

3 tablespoons black bean paste

2 tablespoons Chili Oil (see page 247)

2 tablespoons rice vinegar

2 garlic cloves, minced

1 tablespoon soy sauce

1 teaspoon honey

Scallions, chopped, for garnish

1 To begin preparations for the bowls, cook the rice according to the directions on the package. Fluff the rice with a fork, cover it, and set it aside.

2 Pat the tofu dry with paper towels and dice it. Place the cornstarch in a bowl, season with salt, and dredge the tofu in the mixture until it is completely coated.

3 Place the coconut oil in a large skillet and warm it over medium-high heat. Add the tofu and cook until it is crispy and golden brown, about 8 minutes, turning it as necessary. Add the onion, peppers, and broccoli and cook, stirring occasionally, for 2 minutes.

4 Place the black bean paste, Chili Oil, vinegar, garlic, soy sauce, and honey in a bowl and stir to combine. Gently stir the sauce into the pan and cook for 2 to 3 minutes, tossing to combine.

5 Divide the rice among the serving bowls and top with the tofu and vegetables. Garnish with scallions and serve.

kimchi fried rice

If you have a hankering for Asian flavors, here's an easy recipe to use up leftover rice and any leftover vegetables from the week.

2 tablespoons avocado oil

3 garlic cloves, minced

1 cup sliced mushrooms

½ cup shelled edamame

1 onion, diced

2 tablespoons gochujang

½ cup kimchi

2 to 4 eggs

Salt, to taste

2 cups leftover rice

1 teaspoon sesame oil

Scallions, chopped,
for garnish

Sesame seeds, for garnish

1   Place half of the avocado oil in a large skillet and warm it over medium heat. Add garlic, mushrooms, edamame, and onion and cook, stirring frequently, for 3 minutes.

2   Stir in the gochujang, add the kimchi, and cook, stirring occasionally, for 1 minute.

3   Remove the pan from heat. Place the remaining avocado oil in a separate pan and warm it over medium heat. Add the eggs, season with salt, and fry them until the whites are set and the yolks are to your liking. Set the eggs aside.

4   Add the rice to the pan containing the vegetables and cook over medium heat, without stirring, until it starts to get crispy. Add the sesame oil and toss the fried rice.

5   Divide the fried rice among the serving bowls and top each portion with a fried egg. Garnish with scallions and sesame seeds and serve.

kimchi fried rice,
see page 51

yield: 4 servings / active time: 20 minutes / total time: 40 minutes

cauliflower & sweet potato salad

A crunchy, earthy salad that is especially good on those days in late September when you can feel the summer slipping away.

1 Preheat the oven to 425°F. To begin preparations for the salad, place the olive oil, chili powder, garlic powder, onion powder, cumin, and salt in a bowl and whisk to combine. Add the cauliflower and sweet potato and toss to combine. Place the vegetables on a baking sheet in an even layer, place the pan in the oven, and roast until the vegetables are golden brown and tender, 25 to 30 minutes, stirring halfway through.

2 While the vegetables are roasting, cook the quinoa according to the directions on the package. Fluff it with a fork and set it aside.

3 To prepare the dressing, place all of the ingredients in a bowl and whisk to combine.

4 Remove the roasted vegetables from the oven. Divide the quinoa and spinach among the serving bowls and top each portion with some of the roasted vegetables, avocado, goat cheese, and almonds. Drizzle the dressing over the top, garnish with cilantro, and serve.

For the Salad

3 tablespoons extra-virgin olive oil

½ teaspoon chili powder

1 teaspoon garlic powder

1 teaspoon onion powder

1 teaspoon cumin

1 teaspoon kosher salt

1 head of cauliflower, cut into florets

1 sweet potato, peeled and diced

1 cup quinoa

4 cups baby spinach

Flesh of 1 large avocado, sliced

2 tablespoons crumbled goat cheese

¼ cup sliced almonds

Fresh cilantro, chopped, for garnish

For the Dressing

1 tablespoon almond butter

¼ cup tahini paste

2 tablespoons sriracha

1 tablespoon maple syrup

1 teaspoon curry powder

¼ teaspoon kosher salt

2 tablespoons water

Juice of 1 lemon

1 cup rice

1 tablespoon sesame oil

2½ tablespoons soy sauce

3 tablespoons sriracha

1 tablespoon white vinegar

1 tablespoon ketchup

1 tablespoon sugar

1½ tablespoons cornstarch

1 cup plus 2 tablespoons water

2 tablespoons avocado oil

4 garlic cloves, minced

1 small carrot, peeled and diced

1 cup broccoli florets

1 cup thinly sliced mushrooms

1 large red onion, diced

2 bell peppers, stemmed, seeded, and diced

2 dried red chile peppers, stemmed, seeded, and chopped

Scallions, trimmed and chopped on a bias, for garnish

yield: 4 servings / active time: 25 minutes / total time: 40 minutes

vegetables in spicy garlic sauce

Yet another dish that meets at the crossroads of a few cultures, this time Indian and Chinese. Sweet, sour, and spicy, it's sure to dazzle the taste buds.

1   Cook the rice according to the directions on the package. Fluff it, cover it, and set it aside.

2   Place the sesame oil, soy sauce, sriracha, vinegar, ketchup, sugar, cornstarch, and 2 tablespoons of water in a bowl and whisk until well combined. Set the sauce aside.

3   Place the avocado oil in a large skillet and warm it over medium heat. Add the garlic and cook for 1 minute. Add the carrot and broccoli and cook, stirring occasionally, until they have softened, about 5 minutes.

4   Add the mushrooms, onion, and peppers and cook until the onion is translucent, about 3 minutes.

5   Add the sauce and stir to coat. Add the remaining water, bring to a simmer, and cook until the sauce has reduced slightly, about 10 minutes.

6   Divide the rice among the serving bowls and top each portion with some of the vegetables. Garnish with scallions and serve.

yield: 4 servings / active time: 25 minutes / total time: 35 minutes

kung pao tofu

Feel free to increase or reduce the number of chile peppers used here to fit your personal tolerance for heat.

1 cup rice

14 oz. extra-firm tofu, drained

2 tablespoons avocado oil

1 large onion, diced

1 large bell pepper, stemmed, seeded, and diced

3 dried red chile peppers, stemmed, seeded, and diced

2 tablespoons cornstarch

Salt, to taste

½ cup roasted peanuts

2 garlic cloves, minced

1 cup chopped scallions

2 tablespoons Sichuan peppercorns

2 tablespoons soy sauce

1 tablespoon rice vinegar

1 tablespoon dark soy sauce

1 tablespoon hoisin sauce

1 tablespoons sriracha

1 tablespoon sesame oil

1 teaspoon sugar

1. Cook the rice according to the directions on the package. Fluff it, cover it, and set the rice aside.

2. Place the soy sauce, hoisin sauce, vinegar, dark soy sauce, sesame oil, sriracha, and sugar in a bowl and whisk until well combined. Set the sauce aside.

3. Pat the tofu dry and dice it. Place the cornstarch and salt in a bowl and whisk to combine. Add the tofu and toss to coat.

4. Place the avocado oil in a large skillet and warm it over medium heat. Add the tofu and cook, stirring occasionally, until it is browned, 6 to 8 minutes.

5. Add the garlic and peppercorns and cook for 1 minute. Add the scallions, onion, pepper, and chiles and cook, stirring occasionally, until the vegetables start to soften, about 5 minutes. Add the sauce and stir to coat. Cook until everything is warmed through, 2 to 3 minutes.

6. Divide the rice among serving bowls, top each portion with some of the tofu, vegetables, and peanuts, and serve.

For the Bowls

½ lb. rice noodles

1 tablespoon extra-virgin
olive oil

1 large boneless, skinless
chicken breast, pounded thin

½ teaspoon garlic powder

Pinch of kosher salt

6 Persian cucumbers,
finely diced

1 large carrot, peeled and diced

1 cup chopped red cabbage

1 cup shelled, cooked edamame

1 red bell pepper, stemmed,
seeded, and diced

¼ cup roasted peanuts, plus
more for garnish

1 cup chopped scallions

Fresh cilantro, chopped,
for garnish

Lime wedges, for serving

For the Dressing

⅓ cup peanut butter

1 tablespoon maple syrup

1 garlic clove, grated

1 Thai chile pepper, stemmed,
seeded, and minced

1 tablespoon rice vinegar

1 tablespoon sriracha

1 tablespoon soy sauce

2 tablespoons water

Pinch of kosher salt

yield: 2 servings / active time: 20 minutes / total time: 35 minutes

cold noodle salad

The spicy peanut dressing was the impetus for this dish. Once I encountered it, I could not keep from thinking of ways to utilize it, and this refreshing, comforting salad is one of the best dishes that resulted from that obsession.

1 To begin preparations for the bowl, cook the noodles according to the directions on the package. Drain them and let them cool.

2 To prepare the dressing, place all of the ingredients in a bowl and whisk until well combined. Set the dressing aside.

3 Place the olive oil in a skillet and warm it over medium heat. Season the chicken with the garlic powder and salt, add it to the pan, and cook until it is browned on both sides and cooked through, about 10 minutes, turning it over halfway through. Remove the chicken from the pan and let it cool. When it is cool enough to handle, slice the chicken and set it aside.

4 Place the noodles, cucumbers, carrot, cabbage, edamame, bell pepper, peanuts, scallions, and chicken in a salad bowl and toss to combine.

5 Pour the dressing over the salad and toss until combined.

6 Divide the salad among the serving bowls, garnish with cilantro and additional peanuts, and serve with lime wedges.

yield: 4 servings / active time: 20 minutes / total time: 50 minutes

summer pasta salad

Summertime is here! Which means pool parties and backyard barbecues are where this salad is sure to be a hit.

For the Dressing

½ cup extra-virgin olive oil

¼ cup water

¼ cup white vinegar

1 to 2 teaspoons dried oregano

1 teaspoon red pepper flakes

For the Salad

1 lb. pasta

1½ cups cucumber, diced

2 cups cherry tomatoes, halved

1 red onion, sliced thin

2 tablespoons chopped pickled jalapeño chile peppers

1 lb. salami, chopped

1 cup crumbled feta cheese

½ cup chopped fresh parsley

1 To prepare the dressing, place all of the ingredients in a bowl and whisk to combine. Set the dressing aside.

2 To begin preparations for the salad, cook the pasta according to the directions on the package. Drain the pasta and run it under cold water until it is cool.

3 Place the pasta, cucumber, tomatoes, onion, jalapeños, and salami in a salad bowl and toss to combine. Add the dressing and feta and toss to combine.

4 Add the parsley and stir to combine. Cover the salad bowl with plastic wrap and refrigerate the salad for 15 minutes before serving.

chickpea curry

Chickpeas are a natural fit for the ever-versatile curry, turning this bowl into a surefire crowd-pleaser.

2 tablespoons extra-virgin olive oil

1 onion, finely diced

3 garlic cloves, minced

½ teaspoon red pepper flakes, plus more for garnish

½ teaspoon cumin

½ teaspoon turmeric

1 teaspoon kosher salt

2 tablespoons tomato paste

⅓ cup water

1 (14 oz.) can of coconut milk

2 (14 oz.) cans of chickpeas, drained and rinsed

2 cups baby spinach

Fresh cilantro, for garnish

Naan, for serving

Pickled Vegetables (see page 240), for serving

1   Place the olive oil in a medium saucepan and warm it over medium heat. Add the onion and cook, stirring occasionally, until it just starts to brown, about 8 minutes. Stir in the garlic, red pepper flakes, cumin, turmeric, salt, and tomato paste and cook, stirring continually, for 2 minutes.

2   Add the water and coconut milk and bring to a boil.

3   Add the chickpeas, reduce the heat to medium-low, and simmer the curry for 12 minutes.

4   Stir in the spinach and cook until the curry has thickened.

5   Divide the curry among the serving bowls, garnish with cilantro and additional red pepper flakes, and serve with naan and Pickled Vegetables.

yield: 4 servings / active time: 30 minutes / total time: 40 minutes

tofu tikka masala

I made this for a vegan friend who was visiting me from Australia, and she said it's the best vegan dish she has ever tried! I know that's a bold claim, but just see for yourself.

⅔ cup rice

2 tablespoons avocado oil

14 oz. extra-firm tofu, drained

1 onion, chopped

3 garlic cloves, minced

2 green chile peppers, stemmed, seeded, and diced

3 tablespoons tomato paste

1 tablespoon curry powder

1 teaspoon kosher salt

1 teaspoon garam masala

1 teaspoon cayenne pepper

1 (14 oz.) can of coconut milk

½ cup water

½ cup shredded lettuce

1 cup halved cherry tomatoes

1 cup shredded cabbage

Fresh cilantro, chopped, for garnish

Fresh mint, for garnish

Pickled Red Onion (see page 228), for garnish

1 Cook the rice according to the directions on the package. Fluff it, cover it, and set the rice aside.

2 Place half of the avocado oil in a large skillet over medium heat. Pat the tofu dry and dice it. Add it to the pan and cook, stirring occasionally, until it is golden brown all over, about 8 minutes. Remove the tofu from the pan and set it aside.

3 Add the remaining avocado oil to the skillet and warm it over medium heat. Add the onion and cook, stirring occasionally until the onion starts to brown, about 8 minutes. Add the garlic and chiles and cook, stirring frequently, for 2 minutes.

4 Add the tomato paste, curry powder, salt, garam masala, and cayenne and cook, stirring frequently, for 3 to 4 minutes. Add the coconut milk and water and cook, stirring continually, until the sauce starts to thicken, about 4 minutes.

5 Add the tofu and cook until it is warmed through, about 2 minutes.

6 Divide the rice among the serving bowls and top each portion with some of the tikka masala, lettuce, tomatoes, and cabbage. Garnish with cilantro, mint, and pickled onion and serve.

tofu tikka masala,
see page 65

yield: 4 servings / active time: 20 minutes / total time: 30 minutes

pasta with garden vegetables

This classic dish is a great way to sneak veggies past your kids.

3 tablespoons extra-virgin olive oil

3 garlic cloves, minced

1 onion, finely diced

Salt, to taste

¾ lb. pasta

1 red bell pepper, stemmed, seeded, and finely diced

1 cup chopped carrots

1 cup chopped zucchini

⅓ cup Marinara Sauce (see page 230)

1 teaspoon red pepper flakes (optional)

1 cup shredded mozzarella cheese

2 tablespoons heavy cream

Fresh basil, for garnish

1 Bring water to a boil in a large saucepan. Place the olive oil in a large skillet and warm it over medium heat. Add the garlic and onion to the skillet and cook, stirring occasionally, until the onion is translucent, about 3 minutes.

2 Add salt and the pasta to the boiling water and cook until the pasta is al dente, 8 to 10 minutes. Reserve ½ cup of the pasta water, drain the pasta, and set it aside.

3 Add the zucchini, pepper, and carrots to the skillet and cook, stirring occasionally, until they start to soften, about 5 minutes. Add the sauce and red pepper flakes (if desired) and cook for 2 minutes.

4 Add the pasta and mozzarella and toss to combine. Stir in the heavy cream and then add pasta water as necessary to get the desired consistency for the sauce.

5 Divide the pasta among the serving bowls, garnish with basil, and serve.

yield: 4 servings / active time: 15 minutes / total time: 25 minutes

creamy mushroom spaghetti

From my experience, mushrooms are divisive, and people either love them or hate them. This recipe is sure to transform the latter into the former.

1 tablespoon unsalted butter

1 tablespoon extra-virgin olive oil

5 oz. mushrooms

½ teaspoon kosher salt, plus more to taste

¾ lb. spaghetti

½ teaspoon black pepper

1 teaspoon red pepper flakes

3 garlic cloves, minced

½ cup white wine

½ cup heavy cream

Parmesan cheese, grated, for garnish

Fresh parsley, chopped, for garnish

1. Bring water to a boil in a large saucepan. Place the butter and olive oil in a large skillet and warm it over medium heat. Add the mushrooms to the skillet and cook until they start to brown, about 10 minutes.

2. Add salt and the pasta to the boiling water and cook until the pasta is al dente, 8 to 10 minutes. Reserve ½ cup of the pasta water, drain the pasta, and set it aside.

3. Add the salt, pepper, red pepper flakes, and garlic to the skillet and stir for 1 minute. Deglaze the pan with the wine, scraping up any browned bits from the bottom of the pan.

4. Add the cream and pasta and toss to combine. Add pasta water as necessary to get the desired consistency for the sauce.

5. Divide the pasta among the serving bowls, garnish with Parmesan and parsley, and serve.

roasted tomato soup

Once you've tried this homemade tomato soup, you will never go back to the canned version.

2 lbs. Roma tomatoes, halved

2 small yellow onions, sliced thin

6 garlic cloves, left whole

3 tablespoons extra-virgin olive oil

1 teaspoon kosher salt

1 teaspoon black pepper

4 cups Vegetable Stock (see page 231)

⅓ cup heavy cream

Parmesan cheese, grated, for garnish

Fresh basil, for garnish

Red pepper flakes, for garnish

1 Preheat the oven to 400°F. Place the tomatoes, onions, and garlic on a baking sheet, drizzle the olive oil over them, and season with the salt and pepper. Toss to combine and place the pan in the oven. Roast the vegetables until they are browned and tender, about 30 minutes.

2 Remove the vegetables from the oven and place them in a large pot. Add the stock and cream and puree the mixture with an immersion blender.

3 Bring the soup to a simmer over low heat and cook for 10 minutes.

4 Ladle the soup into warmed bowls, garnish with Parmesan, basil, and red pepper flakes, and serve.

roasted tomato soup,
see page 71

yield: 2 servings / active time: 30 minutes / total time: 45 minutes

karahi paneer

A karahi is a thick, circular, and deep cooking pot that is similar in shape to a wok. It originated in the Indian subcontinent and is now used in Indian, Nepalese, Sri Lankan, Pakistani, Bengali, Afghan, and Caribbean cuisines. This dish would traditionally be prepared in one, but a standard skillet will do.

1   Warm a large skillet over medium heat. Add the coriander seeds, cumin seeds, and chiles and toast them for 1 minute, shaking the pan occasionally. Using a mortar and pestle, grind the mixture into a fine powder.

2   Place half of the avocado oil in a large skillet and warm it over medium heat. Add the ginger and garlic and cook, stirring frequently, for 2 minutes.

3   Add the onion and cook, stirring occasionally, until the onion starts to brown, 6 to 8 minutes.

4   Stir in the tomatoes, tomato paste, turmeric, coriander, salt, and chili powder and cook, stirring frequently, for 2 minutes. Add the water and cook, stirring continually, until the sauce thickens slightly, about 4 minutes. Add the cream and reduce the heat to medium-low.

5   Place the remaining avocado oil in a separate pan and warm it over medium heat. Add the paneer and cook, stirring occasionally, for 3 minutes. Sprinkle the toasted spice mixture over the paneer, add the pepper, and cook for 1 minute.

6   Add the paneer mixture to the sauce and gently stir to combine.

7   Divide the paneer among the serving bowls, garnish with cilantro, and serve with naan and Pickled Vegetables.

1 teaspoon coriander seeds

1 teaspoon cumin seeds

3 dried red chile peppers

2 tablespoons avocado oil

1 teaspoon minced fresh ginger

3 garlic cloves, minced

1 large onion, chopped

2 tomatoes, chopped

1 teaspoon tomato paste

½ teaspoon turmeric

1 teaspoon coriander

1 teaspoon kosher salt

1 teaspoon Kashmiri chili powder

¼ cup water

¼ cup heavy cream

1½ cups paneer

1 bell pepper, stemmed, seeded, and sliced

Fresh cilantro, chopped, for garnish

Naan, for serving

Pickled Vegetables (see page 240), for serving

yield: 4 servings / active time: 15 minutes / total time: 25 minutes

crunchy salad with chicken nuggets

Topping a healthy salad with a childhood favorite is a great way to accept that you're a grown-up while also recognizing that it's important to remember that food can be fun.

1½ cups crushed cornflakes

Salt and pepper, to taste

1 lb. lean ground chicken

1 egg

1 tablespoon garlic powder

1 teaspoon paprika

1 teaspoon mustard powder

1 teaspoon red pepper flakes

4 hearts of romaine lettuce, rinsed well, dried, and chopped

½ cup extra-virgin olive oil

¾ cup grated Parmesan cheese

Juice of 1 large lemon

Spicy Mayo (see page 237)

1　Preheat an air fryer to 350°F. Place the cornflakes in a shallow bowl, season with salt and pepper, and stir to combine.

2　Place the chicken, egg, garlic powder, paprika, mustard powder, and red pepper flakes in a bowl, season with salt, and work the mixture with your hands until it is well combined.

3　Form the mixture into nuggets and dredge them in the cornflake mixture until completely coated.

4　Coat the air fryer tray with nonstick cooking spray and place the nuggets in the tray, working in batches if necessary to avoid overcrowding. Cook the nuggets until they are golden brown and cooked through, 12 to 14 minutes, turning them over halfway through.

5　While the nuggets are cooking, place the lettuce, olive oil, Parmesan, and lemon juice in a bowl and toss to combine.

6　Divide the salad among the serving bowls and top each portion with some of the chicken nuggets. Drizzle the Spicy Mayo over the top and serve.

yield: 4 servings / active time: 10 minutes / total time: 10 minutes

easy chickpea salad

We all have those nights when we are running low on time and energy and are absolutely famished. This dish, which is built around pantry staples, is perfect for such moments.

For the Salad

2 (14 oz.) can of chickpeas, drained and rinsed

2 large cucumbers, chopped

1 red onion, sliced thin

1 red bell pepper, stemmed, seeded, and diced

1 orange bell pepper, stemmed, seeded, and diced

1 yellow bell pepper, stemmed, seeded, and diced

½ cup finely chopped fresh parsley

8 black olives, pitted and chopped (optional)

Feta cheese, crumbled, for garnish (optional)

For the Dressing

¼ cup extra-virgin olive oil

Juice of 1 small lemon

1 teaspoon red pepper flakes

1 teaspoon sugar

Salt, to taste

1 To begin preparations for the salad, place all of the ingredients, except for the feta, in a salad bowl and toss to combine.

2 To prepare the dressing, place all of the ingredients in a bowl and whisk to combine.

3 Add the dressing to the salad and toss to combine. Garnish with feta, if desired, and serve.

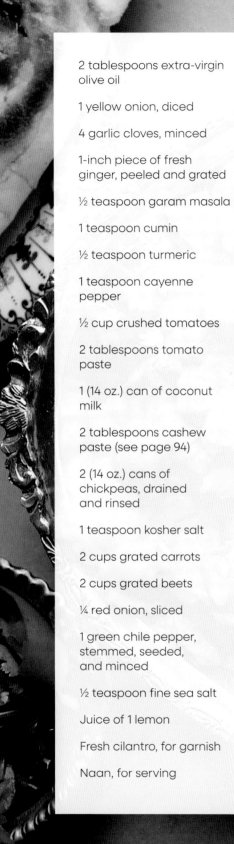

- 2 tablespoons extra-virgin olive oil

- 1 yellow onion, diced

- 4 garlic cloves, minced

- 1-inch piece of fresh ginger, peeled and grated

- ½ teaspoon garam masala

- 1 teaspoon cumin

- ½ teaspoon turmeric

- 1 teaspoon cayenne pepper

- ½ cup crushed tomatoes

- 2 tablespoons tomato paste

- 1 (14 oz.) can of coconut milk

- 2 tablespoons cashew paste (see page 94)

- 2 (14 oz.) cans of chickpeas, drained and rinsed

- 1 teaspoon kosher salt

- 2 cups grated carrots

- 2 cups grated beets

- ¼ red onion, sliced

- 1 green chile pepper, stemmed, seeded, and minced

- ½ teaspoon fine sea salt

- Juice of 1 lemon

- Fresh cilantro, for garnish

- Naan, for serving

creamy chickpeas & root vegetables

Butter chicken, the famous Indian dish, is the inspiration for this vegan-friendly recipe.

1 Place the olive oil in a large skillet and warm it over medium heat. Add the onion and cook, stirring occasionally, until it starts to soften, about 5 minutes.

2 Add the garlic and ginger and cook, stirring frequently, for 1 minute.

3 Stir in the garam masala, cumin, turmeric, cayenne, and salt and cook for 1 minute. Add the tomato paste and tomatoes and cook, stirring occasionally, for 6 minutes.

4 Stir in the coconut milk and cashew paste, add the chickpeas, and simmer until the flavor has developed to your liking, about 8 minutes.

5 While the chickpeas are simmering, place all of the remaining ingredients, except for the cilantro and naan, in a bowl and toss to combine.

6 Divide the carrot-and-beet mixture among the serving bowls. Top each portion with the chickpea mixture, garnish with cilantro, and serve with naan.

vegetarian ramen

These comforting bowls are packed with vegetables, spice, and umami.

1 tablespoon avocado oil

4 garlic cloves, minced

1 tablespoon grated
fresh ginger

4 oz. shiitake mushrooms,
stemmed and chopped

4 cups Vegetable Stock
(see page 231)

2 cups water

1 tablespoon light
soy sauce

4 eggs, left whole

½ lb. ramen noodles

1 cup thinly sliced scallions

1 carrot, peeled and
julienned

2 tablespoons Chili Oil
(see page 247)

1 cup daikon radish,
julienned

1 Place the avocado oil in a large pot and warm it over medium heat. Add the garlic and ginger and cook for 1 minute.

2 Add the mushrooms and stir-fry for 1 minute. Add the stock and water and bring to a boil. Reduce the heat so that the broth simmers and cook for 10 minutes.

3 While the broth is simmering, place the eggs in a large saucepan and cover them with cold water. Bring the water to boil and cook the eggs for another minute.

4 Remove the pan from heat, cover the pan with a lid, and let the eggs rest for 8 minutes. Remove the eggs from the pan, peel them, and set them aside.

5 Stir the noodles into the broth and cook until they are al dente, 2 to 4 minutes. Add the scallions and carrots and cook, stirring occasionally, for 2 minutes.

6 Divide the ramen among the serving bowls, top each portion with a hard-boiled egg and some of the Chili Oil and radish, and serve.

yield: 4 servings / active time: 20 minutes / total time: 1 hour and 30 minutes

harissa chicken salad

A great nutriet-dense salad that has an eye-opening kick from the harissa.

For the Salad

1 tablespoon extra-virgin olive oil

2 tablespoons Harissa Sauce (see page 229)

1 teaspoon garlic powder

½ teaspoon kosher salt

1 teaspoon cumin

3 chicken breasts

4 cups spring mix

¼ cup Pickled Red Onion (see page 228)

2 cups canned corn, drained

4 pitted dates, chopped

Flesh of 2 avocados, diced

2 cups diced cucumber

For the Vinaigrette

⅓ cup extra-virgin olive oil

Juice of 1 lemon

2 garlic cloves, minced

1 shallot, grated

1 teaspoon maple syrup

1 teaspoon kosher salt

1 To begin preparations for the salad, place the olive oil, harissa, garlic powder, salt, and cumin in a mixing bowl and whisk to combine. Add the chicken, turn to coat, and let it marinate it in the refrigerator for 1 hour.

2 To prepare the vinaigrette, place all of the ingredients, except for the olive oil, in a bowl and whisk to combine. While whisking continually, add the olive oil in a slow stream until it has emulsified.

3 Warm a grill pan over medium heat. Add the chicken and cook until it is browned on both sides and cooked through (the interior is 165°F), about 10 minutes, turning it over halfway through. Remove the chicken from the pan and let it cool.

4 Slice the chicken against the grain. Divide the spring mix among the serving bowls, top each portion with some of the chicken, pickled onion, corn, dates, avocado, cucumber, and vinaigrette, and serve.

paneer fries with salad

When you are looking for a healthy meal that does not compromise on flavor, turn to these bowls.

1 tablespoon cornstarch

1 teaspoon kosher salt

½ teaspoon turmeric

1 teaspoon Kashmiri chili powder

½ teaspoon cumin seeds

1 tablespoon ginger-garlic paste

¼ teaspoon ajwain

2 tablespoons water

6 oz. paneer, cut into thin slices

¼ cup avocado oil

Quick Pickled Salad (see page 241)

Chaat masala, for garnish

Fresh cilantro, chopped, for garnish

Mint Chutney (see page 247), for serving

1   Place the cornstarch, salt, turmeric, chili powder, cumin seeds, ginger-garlic paste, ajwain, and water in a bowl and stir the mixture until it is a paste. Add the paneer and gently turn it in the paste until it is completely coated. Marinate the paneer in the refrigerator for 15 minutes.

2   Place the avocado oil in a large skillet and warm it over medium heat. Add the paneer and fry until it is golden brown all over, about 10 minutes, turning it as needed. Remove the paneer fries from the pan and set them on a paper towel–lined plate to drain.

3   Divide the salad among the serving bowls and top each portion with some of the paneer fries. Garnish with chaat masala and cilantro and serve with Mint Chutney.

paneer fries with salad,
see page 85

yield: 4 servings / active time: 20 minutes / total time: 30 minutes

peas pulao

A great one-pot meal that can work on its own or as the foundation for a bowl featuring seafood or poultry.

2 tablespoons ghee

1 teaspoon cumin seeds

1 small onion, chopped

Pinch of kosher salt

½ teaspoon turmeric

1 cup frozen peas

1½ cups Chicken Stock (see page 227)

¾ cup rice

1   Place the ghee in a medium saucepan and warm it over medium heat. Add the cumin seeds, cook for 15 seconds, and then add the onion. Cook, stirring occasionally, until it is translucent, about 3 minutes.

2   Stir in the salt and turmeric and then add the peas, stock, and rice. Stir to combine and bring to a boil. Cover the pan with a lid, reduce the heat to medium-low, and cook until the rice is tender, 7 to 10 minutes.

3   Divide the pulao among the serving bowls and enjoy.

yield: 1 to 2 servings / active time: 10 minutes / total time: 15 minutes

quick summer salad

If you need one more side option for a party at the last minute, this salad is an outstanding bet, as it will pair well with almost anything.

For the Vinaigrette

¼ cup extra-virgin olive oil

¼ cup white vinegar

1 teaspoon kosher salt

1 teaspoon red pepper flakes

1 teaspoon sugar

For the Salad

Kernels from 3 ears of corn

1 English cucumber, sliced

1 large red bell pepper, stemmed, seeded, and chopped

2 cups cherry tomatoes, halved

1 small red onion, sliced thin

Fresh parsley, chopped, for garnish

1 To prepare the vinaigrette, place all of the ingredients in a small bowl and whisk to combine. Set it aside.

2 To begin preparations for the salad, bring water to a boil in a medium saucepan. Add the corn and cook until it turns bright yellow, 3 to 4 minutes. Drain the corn and let it cool completely.

3 Place the cucumber, corn, pepper, cherry tomatoes, and onion in a bowl and toss to combine. Add the dressing and toss to coat.

4 Divide the salad among the serving bowls, garnish with parsley, and serve.

quick summer salad,
see page 89

yield: 4 servings / active time: 25 minutes / total time: 25 minutes

taco salad

I can never get enough of some flavors, and those contained in this salad are examples. If you prefer kidney beans, feel free to swap them in for the black beans.

1 tablespoon chili powder

½ teaspoon ground oregano

½ teaspoon garlic powder

½ teaspoon onion powder

½ teaspoon kosher salt

½ teaspoon cumin

½ teaspoon red pepper flakes

½ teaspoon paprika

1 tablespoon avocado oil

1 onion, finely diced

2 cups canned black beans

1 red bell pepper, stemmed, seeded, and chopped

4 cups chopped lettuce

1 cup canned corn, drained

2 cups chopped cucumbers

½ cup diced cherry tomatoes

½ cup crushed tortilla chips

½ cup shredded Mexican-style cheese

Cilantro Sauce (see page 236)

1. Place the chili powder, oregano, garlic powder, onion powder, kosher salt, cumin, red pepper flakes, and paprika in a small bowl and stir to combine. Set the seasoning blend aside.

2. Place the avocado oil in a large skillet and warm it over medium heat. Add the onion and cook, stirring occasionally, until it is translucent, about 3 minutes.

3. Add the beans, 1 tablespoon of the seasoning blend, and a splash of water and cook, stirring occasionally, for 5 minutes. Store the remaining seasoning blend in a small mason jar.

4. Add the pepper and cook, stirring occasionally, until it has softened, about 5 minutes.

5. Divide the lettuce among the serving bowls, top each portion with some of the bean mixture, corn, cucumbers, tomatoes, tortilla chips, cheese, and sauce, and serve.

yield: 2 servings / active time: 25 minutes / total time: 25 minutes

mushroom masala

By now, you have probably heard about all of the health benefits mushrooms provide. These flavorful bowls are a great way to capitalize on those advantages.

¾ cup cashews

2 tablespoons extra-virgin olive oil

1 onion, chopped

1 teaspoon minced fresh ginger

3 garlic cloves, minced

¾ cup tomato puree

¼ teaspoon turmeric

½ teaspoon cumin

1 teaspoon coriander

1 teaspoon kosher salt

1 teaspoon Kashmiri chili powder

1 lb. white mushrooms, stemmed and sliced

Pickled Red Onion (see page 228)

Fresh cilantro, chopped, for garnish

Naan, for serving

1 Place the cashews in a bowl, cover them with warm water, and let them soak for 5 minutes. Drain the cashews, place them in a blender, and puree until smooth, adding water as needed. Set the cashew paste aside.

2 Place the olive oil in a large skillet and warm it over medium heat. Add the onion and cook, stirring occasionally, until it is translucent, about 3 minutes.

3 Add the ginger and garlic and cook for 1 minute. Stir in the tomato puree, turmeric, cumin, coriander, salt, and chili powder and cook for 2 minutes.

4 Add the mushrooms and cook until the sauce has thickened, about 8 minutes.

5 Remove the pan from heat and stir in 3 tablespoons of the cashew paste.

6 Divide the mushroom masala among the serving bowls and top each portion with some pickled onion. Garnish with cilantro and serve with naan.

easy detox salad

After all of the recipe testing and eating out at restaurants that my week is usually comprised of, there are days when I want something nourishing that helps detox from it all.

For the Dressing

2 tablespoons extra-virgin olive oil

1 tablespoon maple syrup

1 garlic clove, grated

1 teaspoon red pepper flakes

1 tablespoon white vinegar

½ teaspoon kosher salt

Juice of 1 lemon

For the Salad

2 cups finely diced cucumbers

1 cup chopped beets

1 red onion, chopped

1 red bell pepper, stemmed, seeded, and chopped

1 cup cherry tomatoes, halved

1 large carrot, peeled and chopped

¼ cup roasted peanuts

2 cups chopped lettuce

2 tablespoons chopped fresh cilantro

¼ cup roasted sunflower seeds

1 To prepare the dressing, place all of the ingredients in a bowl and whisk until well combined. Set the dressing aside.

2 To prepare the salad, place all of the ingredients, except for the sunflower seeds, in a salad bowl and toss to combine. Add the dressing and toss to combine.

3 Divide the salad among the serving bowls, top each portion with some of the sunflower seeds, and serve.

yield: 4 servings / active time: 15 minutes / total time: 35 minutes

edamame & quinoa salad

This dish came out of a desire to make something delicious that contained all of the healthy stuff I wanted my toddler to eat—sans the hot sauce—and it worked like a charm.

For the Salad

1 cup quinoa

3 cups chopped broccoli

1 cup finely diced red cabbage

½ cup thinly sliced red onion

1 cup cooked edamame

½ cup roasted cashews

¼ cup chopped fresh cilantro

For the Dressing

¼ cup almond butter

1 tablespoon extra-virgin olive oil

2 tablespoons rice vinegar

1 tablespoon sriracha

1 tablespoon maple syrup

1 tablespoon soy sauce

1 teaspoon grated fresh ginger

1 To begin preparations for the salad, cook quinoa according to the directions on the package.

2 While the quinoa is cooking, prepare the dressing. Place all of the ingredients in a bowl and whisk until well combined. Set the dressing aside.

3 Fluff the quinoa with a fork and place it in a bowl. Add the remaining ingredients and toss to combine.

4 Add the dressing to the salad, toss to coat, and serve.

spicy udon noodles

You will be pleasantly surprised by how the spice here is bundled up in the layers of other flavors in this dish.

1 tablespoon sesame oil

2 garlic cloves, minced

½ lb. mushrooms, sliced

½ lb. udon noodles

1 tablespoon soy sauce

1 teaspoon sambal oelek

1 teaspoon honey

Scallions, chopped, for garnish

Chili Oil (see page 247), for garnish

1 Bring water to a boil in a large saucepan. Place the sesame oil in a large skillet and warm it over medium heat. Add the garlic to the skillet and cook for 2 minutes.

2 Add the mushrooms and cook, stirring occasionally, until they have softened, about 6 minutes.

3 Add the noodles to the boiling water and cook according to the directions on the package. Drain the noodles and set them aside.

4 Stir the soy sauce, sambal oelek, and honey into the skillet and cook for 1 minute. Add the noodles and toss to coat.

5 Divide the noodles among the serving bowls, garnish with scallions and Chili Oil, and serve.

yield: 4 servings / active time: 20 minutes / total time: 45 minutes

chickpea & quinoa bowls

These bowls pair the bigger protein-packed hitters from the vegetarian universe. It's a great preparation to make a double batch of, as it keeps well for a few days and is an outstanding grab-and-go option.

1   Preheat the oven to 425°F. Preheat an air fryer to 350°F. To begin preparations for the bowls, cook the quinoa according to the directions on the package. Fluff the quinoa and set it aside.

2   Place the sweet potato in a bowl, add half of the olive oil, and season with salt. Toss to combine, place the sweet potato on a baking sheet in an even layer, and place it in the oven. Roast until the sweet potato is tender and golden brown, about 25 minutes, stirring halfway through.

3   Place the chickpeas in a bowl, add the chili powder, cumin, sugar, and remaining olive oil, and toss to combine. Place the chickpeas in the air fryer and cook until they are golden brown, about 15 minutes.

4   While the sweet potato and chickpeas are cooking, prepare the dressing. Place all of the ingredients in a bowl and stir to combine. Taste, adjust the seasoning as necessary, and set the dressing aside.

5   Remove the sweet potato from the oven and the chickpeas from the air fryer. Divide the quinoa among the serving bowls, top each portion with some of the sweet potato, chickpeas, raisins, and hemp seeds, and drizzle the dressing over the top. Garnish with pickled onion and parsley and serve.

For the Bowls

1 cup quinoa

1 sweet potato, peeled and chopped

2 tablespoons extra-virgin olive oil

Salt, to taste

2 cups canned chickpeas, drained and rinsed

Pinch of red chili powder

Pinch of cumin

Pinch of sugar

⅓ cup raisins

2 tablespoons hemp seeds

Pickled Red Onion (see page 228), for garnish

Fresh parsley, chopped, for garnish

For the Dressing

1 tablespoon chopped fresh cilantro

1 tablespoon Greek yogurt

1 teaspoon fresh lemon juice

Pinch of caster (superfine) sugar

Salt, to taste

Red pepper flakes, to taste

protein packed

Filled with flavor, comforting yet light, and capable of supplying enough energy to get you through whatever the world throws at you, these bowls are where you turn when you are in need of a meal with substance.

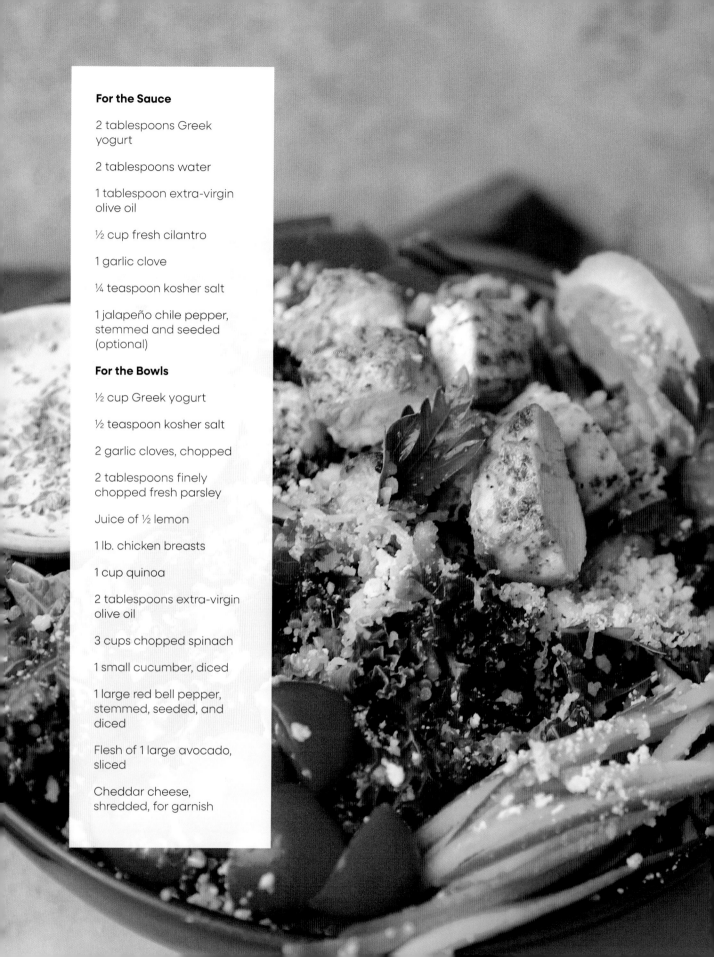

For the Sauce

2 tablespoons Greek yogurt

2 tablespoons water

1 tablespoon extra-virgin olive oil

½ cup fresh cilantro

1 garlic clove

¼ teaspoon kosher salt

1 jalapeño chile pepper, stemmed and seeded (optional)

For the Bowls

½ cup Greek yogurt

½ teaspoon kosher salt

2 garlic cloves, chopped

2 tablespoons finely chopped fresh parsley

Juice of ½ lemon

1 lb. chicken breasts

1 cup quinoa

2 tablespoons extra-virgin olive oil

3 cups chopped spinach

1 small cucumber, diced

1 large red bell pepper, stemmed, seeded, and diced

Flesh of 1 large avocado, sliced

Cheddar cheese, shredded, for garnish

california bowls

Packed with protein and healthy fats, these bowls are perfect after an intense workout or a long hike.

1 To prepare the sauce, place all of the ingredients in a blender and puree until smooth. Set the sauce aside.

2 To begin preparations for the bowls, place the yogurt, salt, garlic, parsley, and lemon juice in a mixing bowl and stir to combine. Add the chicken and stir to coat. Marinate the chicken in the refrigerator for 2 hours.

3 Cook the quinoa according to the directions on the package. Fluff the quinoa with a fork and set it aside.

4 Place the olive oil in a skillet and warm it over medium heat. Add the chicken and cook until it is browned on both sides and cooked through (the interior is 165°F), 8 to 10 minutes. Remove the chicken from the pan and let it rest for 5 minutes.

5 Dice the chicken and set it aside.

6 Divide the quinoa among the serving bowls, add the spinach, cucumber, pepper, avocado, and chicken to each bowl, and top with some of the sauce. Garnish with cheddar and serve.

yield: 4 servings / active time: 20 minutes / total time: 20 minutes

sweet & spicy shrimp stir-fry

This savory and spicy Asian-inspired dish takes the midweek meal to a whole new level, thanks in large part to the homemade Chili Oil.

½ lb. rice noodles

2 tablespoons avocado oil

2 cups chopped scallions

3 garlic cloves, minced

1 large carrot, peeled and finely diced

1 lb. shrimp, shells removed, deveined

1 tablespoon soy sauce

⅓ cup sweet chili sauce

1 large red bell pepper, stemmed, seeded, and diced

⅓ cup crushed peanuts, for garnish

Chili Oil (see page 247), for garnish

Lime wedges, for serving

1 Bring water to a boil in a large saucepan. Add the noodles and cook according to the directions on the package. Drain the noodles and set them aside.

2 Place the avocado oil in a large skillet and warm it over medium-high heat. Add half of the scallions, the garlic, and carrot and cook, stirring occasionally, for 2 minutes.

3 Add the shrimp and cook until it starts to turn pink, 2 to 3 minutes. Add the soy sauce and chili sauce and stir to combine. Add the pepper and cook for 1 minute.

4 Add the noodles and toss to combine. Cook until everything is warmed through and divide the dish among the serving bowls. Garnish with the remaining scallions, the peanuts, and Chili Oil and serve with lime wedges.

Juice of 1 lemon

1 lb. whitefish fillets (tilapia, cod, or halibut), chopped

1 teaspoon kosher salt, plus more to taste

⅔ cup rice

2 to 3 tablespoons avocado oil

1 teaspoon mustard seeds

2 dried red chile peppers, stemmed, seeded, and torn

2 to 4 curry leaves

1 large red onion, pureed

1 tablespoon ginger-garlic paste

½ teaspoon turmeric

½ teaspoon cumin

1 teaspoon coriander

1 teaspoon Kashmiri chili powder

2 large tomatoes, pureed

1 (14 oz.) can of coconut milk

1½ cups water

Pinch of sugar

Fresh cilantro, chopped, for garnish

Lemon wedges, for serving

south indian–style fish curry

A perfect combination of spices coming in hot from South India. Talk about aging well—this dish is hundreds of years old and yet never fails to intrigue.

1 Squeeze half of the lemon juice over the fish and season it with salt. Let the fish marinate in the refrigerator for 30 minutes.

2 Cook the rice according to the directions on the package. Fluff it, cover it, and set it aside.

3 Place the avocado oil in a large skillet and warm it over medium-high heat. Add the mustard seeds, chiles, and curry leaves and cook for 30 seconds.

4 Add the onion and cook until it starts to brown, about 6 minutes. Add ginger-garlic paste, turmeric, cumin, coriander, and chili powder and cook, stirring occasionally, for 1 minute.

5 Stir in the tomatoes and cook for 4 minutes.

6 Add the fish and cook for 3 minutes. Add the coconut milk, remaining lemon juice, water, and sugar and bring to a simmer. Cook until the fish is cooked through, 5 to 7 minutes.

7 Ladle the curry into warmed bowls, garnish with cilantro, and serve with lemon wedges.

yield: 4 servings / active time: 30 minutes / total time: 1 hour

chicken fajita bowls

I had my first fajitas in Austin, Texas, and the dish instantly became a favorite of mine. These bowls are flavorful yet healthy, a combo that is sure to please everyone.

1   To begin preparations for the chicken, place the chicken, half of the avocado oil, onion, bell peppers, garlic, cumin, chili powder, salt, and lemon juice in a bowl, cover it, and marinate the chicken in the refrigerator for 30 minutes.

2   While the chicken is marinating, begin preparations for the bowls. Cook the rice according to the directions on the package and then fluff it. Cover the rice and set it aside.

3   Preheat an air fryer to 350°F.

4   Place the olive oil in a saucepan and warm it over medium heat. Add the onion and garlic and cook, stirring occasionally, until the onion starts to brown, 6 to 7 minutes.

5   Add the salt, black beans, jalapeño, and water, cover the pan, and reduce the heat to medium-low. Cook for 5 minutes, remove the pan from heat, and set the beans aside.

6   Layer the chicken in a single layer in the air fryer and brush it with the remaining avocado oil. Cook until the chicken is browned and cooked through, about 15 minutes, turning it over halfway through.

7   Divide the rice among the serving bowls and top each portion with some of the chicken, black beans, avocado, and tomatoes. Garnish with cilantro and serve with lime wedges.

For the Chicken

1 lb. chicken thighs, trimmed

2 tablespoons avocado oil

1 large onion, sliced

2 bell peppers, stemmed, seeded, and sliced

2 garlic cloves, minced

1 teaspoon cumin

1 teaspoon chili powder

1 teaspoon kosher salt

Juice of ½ lemon

For the Bowls

⅔ cup rice

1 tablespoon extra-virgin olive oil

1 small onion, chopped

2 garlic cloves, minced

¼ teaspoon kosher salt

1 (14 oz.) can of black beans, drained

½ jalapeño chile pepper, diced

⅓ cup water

Flesh of 1 avocado, sliced

⅓ cup halved cherry tomatoes

Fresh cilantro, chopped, for garnish

Lime wedges, for serving

yield: 4 servings / active time: 25 minutes / total time: 25 minutes

beef kebabs

Easy to make, providing ample flavor, and able to work with numerous accompaniments, kebabs are a great centerpiece to build a bowl around.

1 lb. ground beef

1 large onion

1 teaspoon kosher salt

3 garlic cloves, minced

1 teaspoon cumin

1 teaspoon cayenne pepper

2 green chile peppers, stemmed, seeded, and chopped

⅓ cup chopped fresh cilantro

1 egg

2 tablespoons extra-virgin olive oil

1½ cups Labneh (see page 232)

4 Persian cucumbers, sliced

Cilantro Chutney (see page 242)

Sumac Onions (see page 239)

Fresh mint, for garnish

Pita bread, for serving

1   Place the beef in a large bowl and grate the large onion into it. Add the salt, garlic, cumin, cayenne, chiles, cilantro, and egg and work the mixture with your hands until it is well combined. Form heaping tablespoons of the mixture into ovals and set them on a plate. If desired, form the kebabs around skewers.

2   Place the olive oil in a large skillet and warm it over medium heat. Add the kebabs and cook until they are browned all over and cooked through, about 8 minutes. Remove the pan from heat.

3   Spread the Labneh over the bottom of the serving bowls. Top it with some of the kebabs, cucumbers, chutney, and Sumac Onions, garnish with mint, and serve with pitas.

yield: 4 servings / active time: 10 minutes / total time: 10 minutes

spicy honey & garlic shrimp

Anytime you can get a meal with this much flavor on the table this quickly, you've got the makings of a staple weeknight dinner.

1 tablespoon avocado oil

1 lb. jumbo shrimp, shells removed, deveined

⅓ cup chili-garlic sauce

½ teaspoon kosher salt

¼ cup honey

Fresh parsley, chopped, for garnish

Chili Oil (see page 247), for garnish

1   Place the avocado oil in a large skillet and warm it over medium heat. Add the shrimp and cook until it starts to turn pink, 1 to 2 minutes.

2   Turn the shrimp over, add the chili-garlic sauce, honey, and salt, and stir to coat the shrimp. Reduce the heat and cook until the shrimp is cooked through, 1 to 2 minutes.

3   Divide the shrimp among the serving bowls, garnish with parsley and Chili Oil, and serve.

yield: 4 servings / active time: 15 minutes / total time: 20 minutes

coconut shrimp curry

This is one of the simplest recipes in the book, and it comes from my nani, or maternal grandmother. Perhaps it is simply the memories of childhood, but I find this to be a very comforting meal.

⅔ cup white rice

2 tablespoons avocado oil

3 garlic cloves, minced

1 teaspoon ginger paste

1 teaspoon coriander

1 teaspoon Kashmiri chili powder

1 lb. shrimp, shells removed, deveined

Salt, to taste

1 (14 oz.) can of coconut milk

Fresh cilantro, chopped, for garnish

Lemon wedges, for serving

1 Cook the rice according to the directions on the package. Fluff it, cover it, and set the rice aside.

2 Place the avocado oil in a large skillet and warm it over medium heat. Add the garlic and ginger paste and cook for 30 seconds.

3 Stir in the coriander and chili powder and then add the shrimp. Season it with salt and cook until it just starts to turn pink, about 2 minutes.

4 Add the coconut milk and bring to a simmer. Cook until the shrimp is cooked through, about 5 minutes.

5 Divide the shrimp among the serving bowls and ladle the curry over the top. Garnish with cilantro and serve with lemon wedges.

yield: 4 servings / active time: 20 minutes / total time: 25 minutes

spicy salmon bowls

I hope you enjoy the ease of preparation considering the flavor and nutrition available in this preparation.

⅔ cup rice

1½ tablespoons avocado oil

Juice of 1 lime

1 tablespoon garlic powder

1 tablespoon onion powder

2 teaspoons paprika

1 tablespoon Kashmiri chili powder

1 lb. wild salmon fillets, cubed

Smashed Cucumber Salad (see page 244)

Spicy Mayo (see page 237)

2 sheets of nori seaweed, shredded

Sesame seeds, for garnish

1 Cook the rice according to the directions on the package. Fluff it, cover it, and set the rice aside.

2 Place the avocado oil, lime juice, garlic powder, onion powder, paprika, and chili powder in a large bowl and stir to combine. Add the salmon and stir to coat. Let the salmon marinate for 5 minutes.

3 Place the salmon in a large skillet and cook it over medium heat until it is browned and cooked through, 6 to 8 minutes, stirring occasionally.

4 Divide the rice among the serving bowls and top each portion with some of the salmon, Smashed Cucumber Salad, Spicy Mayo, and seaweed. Garnish with sesame seeds and serve.

For the Bowls

3 tablespoons extra-virgin olive oil

1 teaspoon kosher salt

Juice of ½ lemon

4 garlic cloves, minced

½ teaspoon turmeric

½ teaspoon cumin

½ teaspoon cardamom

½ teaspoon cinnamon

1 teaspoon cayenne pepper

½ teaspoon Aleppo pepper

1 lb. boneless, skinless chicken thighs, chopped

3 cups chopped lettuce

2 Persian cucumbers, sliced

Sumac Onions (see page 239)

Fresh parsley, chopped, for garnish

Fresh mint, chopped, for garnish

Pita bread, for serving

For the Sauce

¼ cup Greek yogurt

2 tablespoons mayonnaise

1 garlic clove, grated

¼ teaspoon kosher salt

chicken shawarma

Though traditionally this is made on a rotisserie, which not many people have in their kitchens, I always thought that chicken shawarma was far too flavorful not to try to make at home. After a few attempts, I settled on this delightful version.

1   To begin preparations for the bowls, place 1 tablespoon of olive oil, the salt, lemon juice, garlic, turmeric, cumin, cardamom, cinnamon, cayenne, and Aleppo pepper in a bowl and stir to combine. Add the chicken, stir until it is coated all over, and let it marinate in the refrigerator for 1 hour.

2   Place the remaining olive oil in a large skillet and warm it over medium heat. Add the chicken and cook until it is browned, 4 to 5 minutes. Turn the chicken over, reduce the heat to medium-low, and cook until it is cooked through, about 8 minutes. Remove the pan from heat.

3   To prepare the sauce, place all of the ingredients in a bowl and stir to combine.

4   Divide the lettuce among the serving bowls and top each portion with some of the chicken, cucumbers, Sumac Onions, and sauce. Garnish with parsley and mint and serve with pitas.

easy beef bulgogi

The magic made available by employing gochujang is on full display in these bowls.

For the Beef

1 tablespoon avocado oil

2 shallots, chopped

3 garlic cloves, minced

1 tablespoon grated fresh ginger

1 lb. ground beef

2½ tablespoons soy sauce

3 tablespoons gochujang

1 teaspoon kosher salt

1 tablespoon light brown sugar or honey

For the Bowls

⅔ cup rice

Quick Pickled Salad (see page 241)

⅓ cup kimchi

⅓ cup roasted cashews

1 tablespoon sesame seeds

1 To begin preparations for the bowls, cook the rice according to the directions on the package. Fluff it, cover it, and set the rice aside.

2 To begin preparations for the beef, place the avocado oil in a large skillet and warm it over medium heat. Add the shallots, garlic, and ginger and cook, stirring frequently, for 2 minutes.

3 Add the beef and cook until it starts to brown, about 5 minutes, breaking it up with a wooden spoon.

4 Stir in the soy sauce, gochujang, salt, and brown sugar and cook, stirring occasionally, until the beef is cooked through, about 6 minutes.

5 Divide the rice among the serving bowls, top each portion with some of the beef, pickled salad, kimchi, cashews, and sesame seeds, and serve.

yield: 4 servings / active time: 10 minutes / total time: 25 minutes

sweet & spicy salmon

Between their eye-catching appearance, effortless prep, and considerable flavor, my bet is these bowls become a weekly staple in your house—as they are in mine.

⅔ cup jasmine rice

1 lb. wild salmon fillets, cubed

1 teaspoon kosher salt

1 tablespoon avocado oil

1 tablespoon soy sauce

1 tablespoon minced fresh ginger

3 tablespoons sriracha

1 tablespoon honey

Pickled Vegetables (see page 240)

Sesame seeds, for garnish

Scallions, chopped, for garnish

1 Preheat an air fryer to 400°F. Cook the rice according to the directions on the package. Fluff it, cover it, and set the rice aside.

2 Season the salmon with the salt. Place the avocado oil, soy sauce, ginger, sriracha, and honey in a bowl and stir to combine. Add the salmon and stir to coat.

3 Place the salmon in the air fryer and cook until it is crispy and cooked through, 8 to 10 minutes.

4 Divide the rice among the serving bowls and top each portion with some of the salmon and Pickled Vegetables. Garnish with sesame seeds and scallions and serve.

yield: 4 servings / active time: 20 minutes / total time: 30 minutes

thai basil chicken

Vibrant, savory, spicy, and with a distinct anise note, Thai basil gets the star treatment it deserves in this dish.

½ cup rice

2 tablespoons avocado oil

3 garlic cloves, minced

1 tablespoon minced
fresh ginger

1 lb. ground chicken

3 tablespoons sambal
oelek, or to taste

1 tablespoon oyster sauce

1 tablespoon soy sauce

1 teaspoon sugar

½ teaspoon kosher salt

½ cup water

Juice of 1 lime

1 cup chopped scallions,
plus more for garnish

½ cup fresh Thai basil, plus
more for garnish

2 cups chopped lettuce

¼ cup peanuts

Chili Oil (see page 247),
for garnish)

1 Cook the rice according to the directions on the package. Fluff it, cover it, and set the rice aside.

2 Place the avocado oil in a large skillet and warm it over medium heat. Add the garlic and ginger and cook, stirring frequently, for 2 minutes. Add the chicken and cook until it starts to brown, about 5 minutes, breaking it up with a wooden spoon.

3 Stir in the sambal oelek, oyster sauce, soy sauce, sugar, salt, water, and lime juice. Add the scallions and basil and cook, stirring occasionally, until the chicken is cooked through, about 5 minutes.

4 Divide the rice among the serving bowls and top each portion with some of the lettuce, chicken, and peanuts. Garnish with Chili Oil and additional scallions and basil and serve.

yield: 4 servings / active time: 25 minutes / total time: 40 minutes

chicken fried rice

The simplest of marinades and a bit of Chili Oil help turn a simple bowl of rice into an unforgettable dish.

1 lb. boneless, skinless chicken thighs, chopped

2 tablespoons cornstarch

3 tablespoons soy sauce

2 tablespoons avocado oil

3 garlic cloves, minced

1½ cups chopped scallions

2 green Thai chile peppers, stemmed, seeded, and minced

1½ teaspoons honey

1 teaspoon kosher salt

2 tablespoons Chili Oil (see page 247), plus more for garnish

2 carrots, peeled and finely diced

1 red bell pepper, stemmed, seeded, and chopped

2 cups leftover rice

Sesame seeds, for garnish

1 Place the chicken in a large bowl. Sprinkle the cornstarch over it, add the soy sauce, and stir to coat. Let the chicken marinate for 15 minutes.

2 Place the avocado oil in a large skillet and warm it over medium heat. Add the garlic and 1 cup of scallions and cook, stirring frequently, until the scallions are translucent, about 3 minutes.

3 Add the chicken and cook, stirring occasionally, until it starts to brown, about 5 minutes.

4 Stir in the chiles, honey, and salt and cook until the chicken is cooked through, 3 to 5 minutes. Add a splash of water to the pan if the mixture starts sticking to it.

5 Remove the pan from heat, cover it, and set it aside.

6 Place the Chili Oil in a large skillet and warm it over medium heat.

7 Add the carrots and bell pepper and cook, stirring occasionally, for 4 minutes. Raise the heat to medium-high, add the rice, and cook without stirring until it starts to brown, about 5 minutes.

8 Divide the fried rice among the serving bowls and top each portion with some of the chicken and remaining scallions. Garnish with sesame seeds and additional Chili Oil and serve.

spaghetti & meatballs

When time is short, being able to pop open a jar of store-bought tomato sauce is a godsend, but it can never match the taste of homemade. This version offers the best of both options, and it's amazingly versatile.

For the Meatballs

1½ lbs. ground beef

1 large onion, grated

½ cup bread crumbs

1 teaspoon cayenne pepper

1 teaspoon kosher salt

1 teaspoon oregano

3 garlic cloves, minced

⅓ cup chopped fresh basil

1 egg

2 tablespoons extra-virgin olive oil

For the Sauce

2 tablespoons extra-virgin olive oil

3 garlic cloves, minced

1 teaspoon kosher salt

1 teaspoon red pepper flakes

3 cups halved cherry tomatoes

1½ teaspoons sugar

1 teaspoon dried basil

1 teaspoon white vinegar

1 tablespoon tomato paste

Handful of fresh basil

6 oz. fresh mozzarella cheese, drained and torn

Salt, to taste

½ lb. pasta

Fresh basil, chopped, for garnish

1 To begin preparations for the sauce, place the olive oil in a medium saucepan and warm it over medium heat. Add the garlic and cook for 2 minutes.

2 Add the salt, red pepper flakes, and tomatoes and cook, stirring occasionally, for 5 minutes.

3 Stir in the sugar, dried basil, vinegar, and tomato paste and cover the pan. Cook for 5 minutes.

4 Stir the fresh basil into the sauce. Cook for 1 minute, remove the pan from heat, and set the sauce aside.

5 Preheat the oven to 350°F. To prepare the meatballs, place all of the ingredients, except for the olive oil, in a large bowl and work the mixture with your hands until well combined. Form the mixture into balls and place them on a plate.

6 Place the olive oil in a large skillet and warm it over medium heat. Working in batches to avoid crowding the pan, add the meatballs and cook until they are browned all over, about 6 minutes, turning them as necessary. Transfer the browned meatballs to a baking dish.

7 Pour the sauce over the meatballs, sprinkle the mozzarella over the top, and place the dish in the oven. Bake until the cheese has melted and the meatballs are cooked through, about 20 minutes.

8 While the meatballs are in the oven, bring water to a boil in a large saucepan. Add salt, let the water return to a full boil, and add the pasta. Cook until it is al dente, 8 to 10 minutes. Drain the pasta and set it aside.

9 Remove the meatballs from the oven. Divide the pasta among the serving bowls and top each portion with some of the meatballs. Garnish with basil and serve.

For the Kebabs

1 lb. ground chicken

1 onion, grated

2 garlic cloves, minced

1 teaspoon minced fresh ginger

1 teaspoon cumin

1 tablespoon coriander

1 tablespoon chili powder

¼ cup chopped fresh cilantro

Seeds of 2 cardamom pods

1 teaspoon black pepper

1 teaspoon kosher salt

3 tablespoons avocado oil

For the Salad

2 Persian cucumbers

2 plum tomatoes

1 small onion, diced

2 tablespoons chopped fresh cilantro

½ teaspoon kosher salt

½ teaspoon Kashmiri chili powder

Juice of ½ lemon

Spicy Green Chutney (see page 243), for serving

yield: 4 servings / active time: 30 minutes / total time: 30 minutes

chicken kebab & kachumber salad bowls

There is something so refreshing about the combination of this simple salad and the chutney. Paired with a classic kebab, it is the perfect foundation for a bowl.

1   To begin preparations for the kebabs, place all of the ingredients, except for the avocado oil, in a large bowl and work the mixture until well combined. Working with wet hands, shape the mixture into ovals and thread them onto skewers.

2   Place the avocado oil in a large skillet and warm it over medium heat. Add the kebabs and cook until they are cooked through and golden brown, 8 to 10 minutes, turning them as necessary.

3   Remove the kebabs from the pan, cover them loosely with aluminum foil, and set them aside.

4   To prepare the salad, place all of the ingredients in a mixing bowl and toss to combine.

5   Divide the salad among the serving bowls and top each portion with some of the kebabs. Drizzle some chutney over each portion and serve.

harissa chicken meatballs over couscous

The subtle heat of the harissa, the white sauce, and the couscous really pair well together.

1 To prepare the sauce, place all of the ingredients in a bowl and stir to combine. Set the sauce aside.

2 To begin preparations for the bowls, cook the couscous according to the directions on the package. Drizzle a little olive oil over it and stir to prevent the couscous from sticking. Set it aside.

3 Place the chicken, harissa, cumin, salt, egg, onion, garlic, bread crumbs, and parsley in a bowl and work the mixture with your hands until it is well combined. Form the mixture into balls and place them on a plate.

4 Place the olive oil in a large skillet and warm it over medium heat. Working in batches to avoid crowding the pan, add the meatballs and cook until they are browned all over and cooked through, 8 to 10 minutes, turning them as necessary. Transfer the cooked meatballs to a plate.

5 Divide the couscous among the serving bowls and top each portion with some of the meatballs, sauce, Pickled Vegetables, and raisins. Garnish with herbs and serve.

For the Sauce

2 tablespoons Greek yogurt

1 tablespoon mayonnaise

1 garlic clove, minced

¼ teaspoon kosher salt

For the Bowls

1½ cups pearl couscous

2 tablespoons extra-virgin olive oil, plus more as needed

1 lb. ground chicken

2 tablespoons harissa paste

1 teaspoon cumin

1 teaspoon kosher salt

1 egg

1 large onion, grated

3 garlic cloves, minced

½ cup bread crumbs

⅓ cup chopped fresh parsley

Pickled Vegetables (see page 240)

¼ cup raisins

Fresh herbs, chopped, for garnish

yield: 4 servings / active time: 40 minutes / total time: 1 hour and 40 minutes

butter chicken

One of the most popular and beloved Indian dishes around the globe, butter chicken has it all, containing succulent chicken, an incredible creamy sauce, sweetness, and spice.

For the Bowls

1½ lbs. boneless, skinless chicken thighs, diced

⅓ cup full-fat yogurt

1 teaspoon cumin

1 teaspoon coriander

1 teaspoon Kashmiri chili powder

½ teaspoon turmeric

1 teaspoon ginger paste

1 teaspoon garlic paste

1 tablespoon white vinegar

Salt, to taste

2 tablespoons avocado oil

1 cup rice

2 cucumbers, sliced

Fresh cilantro, chopped, for garnish

Dried fenugreek, for garnish

Naan, for serving

Lemon wedges, for serving

For the Sauce

2 tablespoons unsalted butter

1 bay leaf

Seeds of 2 cardamom pods

1 onion, finely diced

1 teaspoon ginger paste

1 teaspoon garlic paste

2 green Thai chile peppers, stemmed, seeded, and minced

1 tomato, finely diced

1 teaspoon garam masala

1 teaspoon coriander

1 teaspoon Kashmiri chili powder

1 teaspoon honey

3 tablespoons tomato paste

Salt, to taste

½ cup heavy cream

1. To begin preparations for the bowls, place the chicken, yogurt, cumin, coriander, chili powder, turmeric, ginger, garlic, and vinegar in a mixing bowl, season with salt, and stir to combine. Marinate the chicken in the refrigerator for at least 1 hour.

2. Cook the rice according to the directions on the package. Fluff the rice, cover it, and set it aside.

3. Place the avocado oil in a large skillet and warm it over medium-high heat. Add the chicken and cook until it is browned all over and just about cooked through, 8 to 10 minutes, turning it as necessary. Remove the chicken from the pan and set it aside.

4. To begin preparations for the sauce, place the butter in a medium saucepan and melt it over medium heat. Add the bay leaf and cardamom and cook for 30 seconds. Add the onion and cook, stirring occasionally, until it has softened, about 8 minutes. Add the ginger, garlic, chiles, and tomato and cook, stirring frequently, for 2 minutes.

5. Stir in the garam masala, coriander, chili powder, honey, and tomato paste, season with salt, and cook, stirring frequently, until the sauce darkens, about 3 minutes.

6. Stir in the cream and chicken and cook until the chicken is cooked through, 3 to 4 minutes.

7. Divide the rice among the serving bowls and top each portion with some of the butter chicken and cucumbers. Garnish with cilantro and fenugreek and serve with naan and lemon wedges.

butter chicken,
see page 138

yield: 4 servings / active time: 30 minutes / total time: 1 hour and 20 minutes

buddha bowls with chicken

When I crave something healthy and nourishing after a long day, one of these bowls always hits the spot.

1 lb. boneless, skinless chicken breasts

2 garlic cloves, minced

1 tablespoon extra-virgin olive oil

1 teaspoon cayenne pepper

½ teaspoon cumin

1 teaspoon onion powder

Juice of ½ lemon

⅔ cup quinoa

3 tablespoons mayonnaise

3 tablespoons Greek yogurt

1 tablespoon sriracha

2 cups chopped greens

2 Persian cucumbers, sliced

2 handfuls of cherry tomatoes, halved

Flesh of 1 avocado, sliced

Pickled Red Onion (see page 228)

Fresh cilantro, chopped, for garnish

1 Place the chicken, garlic, olive oil, cayenne, cumin, onion powder, and lemon juice in a bowl and stir to combine. Marinate the chicken in the refrigerator for 30 minutes.

2 Cook the quinoa according to the directions on the package. Fluff it, cover it, and set the quinoa aside.

3 Place the mayonnaise, Greek yogurt, and sriracha in a bowl and stir to combine. Set the sauce aside.

4 Place the chicken in a large skillet and cook it over medium heat until it is browned and cooked through, 8 to 10 minutes. Remove the chicken from the pan and let it rest for 2 minutes.

5 Divide the quinoa among the serving bowls and top each portion with some of the greens, cucumbers, tomatoes, avocado, and pickled onion. Slice the chicken and add it to the bowls. Top with the sauce, garnish with cilantro, and serve.

yield: 4 servings / active time: 20 minutes / total time: 1 hour and 20 minutes

chicken tikka masala

An air-fried version of a classic Indian dish that ensures a perfect result every time.

For the Chicken

1 lb. boneless, skinless chicken thighs, chopped

½ cup yogurt

1 tablespoon ginger-garlic paste

1 tablespoon cayenne pepper

½ teaspoon cumin

½ teaspoon turmeric

2 tablespoons extra-virgin olive oil, plus more as needed

1 teaspoon kosher salt

Juice of ½ lemon

For the Salad

2 cups shredded carrots

2 cups shredded beets

1 red onion, sliced

1 green chile pepper, stemmed, seeded, and diced

Juice of 1 lemon

½ teaspoon kosher salt

Fresh cilantro, chopped, for garnish

Mint Chutney (see page 247), for serving

1 To begin preparations for the chicken, place all of the ingredients in a mixing bowl and stir to combine. Marinate the chicken in the refrigerator for 1 hour.

2 While the chicken is marinating, prepare the salad. Place all of the ingredients in a mixing bowl and toss to combine. Set the salad aside.

3 Preheat an air fryer to 350°F. Place the chicken in the air fryer, brush it with olive oil, and cook until it is cooked through, about 15 minutes, turning it over halfway through.

4 Divide the salad among the serving bowls and top each portion with some of the chicken. Garnish with cilantro and serve with Mint Chutney.

yield: 4 servings / active time: 20 minutes / total time: 30 minutes

chicken & rice, south indian style

A simple, hearty recipe that has tons of flavor thanks to the curry leaves, mustard seeds, and spice blend.

1   Cook the rice according to the directions on the package. Fluff it, cover it, and set the rice aside.

2   Place the avocado oil in a large saucepan and warm it over medium heat. Add the mustard seeds, curry leaves, and chiles and stir-fry for 15 seconds. Add the onion, garlic, and ginger and cook, stirring frequently, until the onion starts to brown, about 6 minutes.

3   Stir in the turmeric, cumin, coriander, and chili powder and season with salt. Add tomato paste and a splash of water and cook, stirring continually, for 2 minutes.

4   Raise the heat to medium-high, add the chicken, and cook until the chicken is browned all over, 6 to 8 minutes, stirring frequently.

5   Add the coconut milk and water and bring the dish to a simmer. Cover the pan and cook until the chicken is cooked through and the broth has thickened slightly, about 10 minutes.

6   Divide the rice among the serving bowls and top each portion with some of the chicken and broth. Garnish with cilantro and additional curry leaves and serve.

⅔ cup rice

2 tablespoons avocado oil

1½ teaspoons mustard seeds

12 curry leaves, plus more for garnish

2 dried red chile peppers, stemmed, seeded, and minced

1 onion, finely diced

3 garlic cloves, minced

1 teaspoon minced fresh ginger

½ teaspoon turmeric

½ teaspoon cumin

1 teaspoon coriander

½ teaspoon Kashmiri chili powder

Salt, to taste

2 tablespoons tomato paste

1 lb. boneless, skinless chicken thighs, chopped

1 (14 oz.) can of coconut milk

¼ cup water

Fresh cilantro, chopped, for garnish

yield: 4 servings / active time: 25 minutes / total time: 40 minutes

chicken patties & slaw

A little bit of inspiration from the Far East helped me come up with this flavorful bowl, which is packed with delicious flavors, crunch, and satisfaction.

1 lb. ground chicken

1 egg

2 tablespoons sambal oelek

1 cup chopped scallions, plus more for garnish

3 garlic cloves, minced

1 teaspoon kosher salt

1 tablespoon soy sauce

1 tablespoon fish sauce

2 tablespoons extra-virgin olive oil

3 cups shredded cabbage

2 cups shredded carrots

1 red onion, thinly sliced

Peanut Sauce (see page 239)

Roasted peanuts, chopped, for garnish

1   Place the chicken, egg, sambal oelek, scallions, garlic, salt, soy sauce, and fish sauce in a bowl and work the mixture with your hands until combined. Form the mixture until patties.

2   Place the olive oil in a large skillet and warm it over medium heat. Working in batches to avoid crowding the pan, add the patties and cook until they are cooked through and browned all over, turning them as necessary, 8 to 10 minutes. Transfer the chicken patties to a plate.

3   Place the cabbage, carrots, and onion in a mixing bowl and toss to combine. Add the sauce and toss to combine.

4   Divide the slaw among the serving bowls and top each portion with some of the chicken patties. Garnish with peanuts and additional scallions and serve.

yield: 4 servings / active time: 20 minutes / total time: 25 minutes

turkey lettuce wraps

These light, refreshing wrap-bowl hybrids are great for any day of the week and any time of the day.

For the Sauce

1 tablespoon fish sauce

3 tablespoons soy sauce

3 tablespoons sweet chili sauce

3 garlic cloves, minced

1 tablespoon rice vinegar

2½ tablespoons hoisin sauce

For the Bowls

2 tablespoons avocado oil

1 tablespoon minced fresh ginger

3 garlic cloves, minced

1 lb. ground turkey

1 teaspoon kosher salt

1 red bell pepper, stemmed, seeded, and finely diced

1 cup chopped scallions

Leaves from 2 heads of butter lettuce, rinsed well and separated

1 To prepare the sauce, place all of the ingredients in a bowl and whisk until combined. Set the sauce aside.

2 To begin preparations for the bowls, place the avocado oil in a large skillet and warm it over medium heat. Add the ginger and garlic and cook for 1 minute. Add the turkey and salt cook until it is browned, about 6 minutes, breaking it up with a wooden spoon.

3 Add the pepper and cook for 2 minutes. Pour the sauce over the turkey and cook, stirring occasionally, until it is cooked through, about 4 minutes.

4 Stir in the scallions and cook until the sauce starts to thicken.

5 Arrange the lettuce leaves in the serving bowls. Top each portion with some of the turkey and serve.

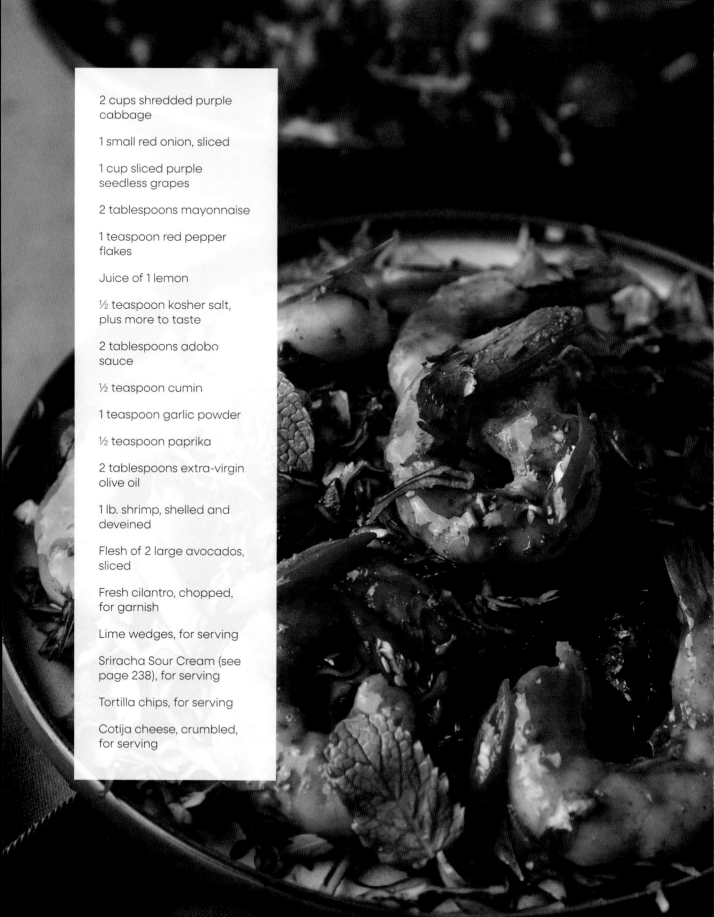

2 cups shredded purple cabbage

1 small red onion, sliced

1 cup sliced purple seedless grapes

2 tablespoons mayonnaise

1 teaspoon red pepper flakes

Juice of 1 lemon

½ teaspoon kosher salt, plus more to taste

2 tablespoons adobo sauce

½ teaspoon cumin

1 teaspoon garlic powder

½ teaspoon paprika

2 tablespoons extra-virgin olive oil

1 lb. shrimp, shelled and deveined

Flesh of 2 large avocados, sliced

Fresh cilantro, chopped, for garnish

Lime wedges, for serving

Sriracha Sour Cream (see page 238), for serving

Tortilla chips, for serving

Cotija cheese, crumbled, for serving

yield: 4 servings / active time: 15 minutes / total time: 15 minutes

spicy shrimp with cabbage & grape slaw

From the cabbage to the grapes and shrimp, this bowl is positively packed with freshness and crunch.

1 Place the cabbage, onion, and grapes in a bowl. Add the mayonnaise, red pepper flakes, and lemon juice, season with salt, and toss to combine. Chill the slaw in the refrigerator.

2 Place the adobo sauce, cumin, garlic powder, paprika, salt, and olive oil in a bowl and stir to combine. Add the shrimp and toss to coat.

3 Place the shrimp in a large skillet and cook them over medium heat until they have turned pink and are cooked through, 3 to 4 minutes, turning them over halfway through. Remove the pan from heat.

4 Divide the slaw among the serving bowls and top each portion with the some of the shrimp and avocado. Garnish with cilantro and serve with lime wedges, sour cream, tortilla chips, and cotija.

tuna lettuce wraps

After a particularly indulgent weekend, all I want is a light, refreshing meal. These crunchy, low-carb wraps filled with tuna fit the bill. One thing: use shallow bowls for serving, as they will make it much easier to put everything together.

2 (5 oz.) cans of tuna, drained

⅓ cup mayonnaise

1 small red onion, chopped

2 tablespoons chopped pickled jalapeño chile peppers

2 teaspoons whole-grain mustard

2 tablespoons chopped fresh parsley, plus more for garnish

½ teaspoon kosher salt

1 teaspoon black pepper

Leaves from 1 head of butter lettuce, rinsed well and separated

1 Place all of the ingredients, except for the lettuce, in a mixing bowl and stir until well combined.

2 Arrange the lettuce in the serving bowls. Top each portion with some of the tuna mixture, garnish with parsley, and serve.

yield: 4 servings / active time: 20 minutes / total time: 30 minutes

chicken & broccoli

These bowls are informed by one of my favorite Chinese takeout dishes. The key is the Shaoxing wine, as it provides the authentic flavor I'm looking for.

1 cup jasmine rice

4 cups broccoli florets

3 tablespoons soy sauce

3 tablespoons oyster sauce

1 tablespoon sesame oil

1 cup water

2 tablespoons cornstarch

1½ tablespoons Shaoxing wine

2 tablespoons avocado oil

3 garlic cloves, minced

1 small onion, chopped

1 lb. boneless, skinless chicken thighs, chopped

1 Cook the rice according to the directions on the package. Fluff it, cover it, and set it aside.

2 Bring a few inches of water to a simmer in a medium saucepan. Place the broccoli in a steaming basket, place it over the simmering water, and cook until it is just tender. Set the broccoli aside.

3 Place the soy sauce, oyster sauce, Shaoxing wine, sesame oil, water, and cornstarch in a bowl and whisk until combined. Set the sauce aside.

4 Place the avocado oil in a large skillet and warm it over medium heat. Add the garlic and onion and cook, stirring frequently, for 2 minutes.

5 Add the chicken and cook until it is browned all over, about 5 minutes, turning it as necessary.

6 Add the broccoli and sauce and stir until well combined. Cook until the chicken is cooked through, about 5 minutes.

7 Divide the rice among the serving bowls, top each portion with some of the chicken and broccoli, and serve.

yield: 4 servings / active time: 20 minutes / total time: 45 minutes

quick chicken bolognese

Everybody loves Italian food, which is how I ended up with a whole bunch of pasta-based bowls.

2 tablespoons extra-virgin olive oil

3 garlic cloves, minced

1 onion, finely diced

1 lb. ground chicken

Salt and pepper, to taste

1 teaspoon red pepper flakes

3 cups Marinara Sauce (see page 230)

¾ lb. pasta

Parmesan cheese, grated, for garnish

Fresh basil, for garnish

1 Bring water to a boil in a large saucepan. Place the olive oil in a large skillet and warm it over medium heat. Add the garlic and onion to the skillet and cook, stirring occasionally, until the onion is translucent, about 3 minutes.

2 Add the chicken, season with salt, pepper, and the red pepper flakes, and cook until the chicken is browned, about 6 minutes, breaking it up with a wooden spoon.

3 Add the sauce and bring to a simmer. Reduce the heat to medium-low and simmer for 15 minutes.

4 Add salt and the pasta to the boiling water and cook until the pasta is al dente, 8 to 10 minutes. Reserve ½ cup of the pasta water, drain the pasta, and set it aside.

5 Add the pasta to the sauce and toss to combine. Add pasta water as necessary to get the desired consistency for the sauce.

6 Divide the pasta among the serving bowls, garnish with Parmesan and basil, and serve.

cauliflower tabbouleh & chicken meatballs

I had made each of these components on separate nights and got the sneaky feeling they would go well together. Sure enough, they are perfectly complementary, so much so that no one suspected the delicious dinner was just a happy accident.

For the Sauce

½ cup fresh mint

½ teaspoon cumin

¼ teaspoon kosher salt

Pinch of sugar

1 garlic clove

Juice of ½ lemon

For the Tabbouleh

2 tablespoons extra-virgin olive oil

3 cups grated cauliflower

1 cup cherry tomatoes, halved

1 cup sliced Persian cucumbers

2 tablespoons finely chopped fresh cilantro

2 tablespoons finely chopped fresh parsley

Juice of ½ lemon

½ teaspoon kosher salt

For the Meatballs

1 lb. ground chicken

1 onion, grated

2 tablespoons avocado oil, plus more as needed

2 garlic cloves, minced

1 teaspoon cumin

1 teaspoon red pepper flakes

¼ cup chopped fresh cilantro

1 teaspoon black pepper

1 teaspoon kosher salt

½ cup crumbled feta cheese

1 egg

1 To prepare the sauce, place all of the ingredients in a blender and puree until smooth. Set the sauce aside.

2 To begin preparations for the tabbouleh, place the olive oil in a large skillet and warm it over medium heat. Add the cauliflower and cook, stirring occasionally, until it is tender, 6 to 8 minutes. Remove the pan from heat and let it cool.

3 Place the tomatoes, cucumbers, cilantro, parsley, and lemon juice in a bowl and stir to combine. Stir in the cauliflower and salt and set the tabbouleh aside.

4 To begin preparations for the meatballs, place all of the ingredients in a bowl and work the mixture with your hands until well combined. Form the mixture into 1-inch meatballs.

5 Coat a large skillet with avocado oil and add the meatballs, working in batches if necessary to avoid crowding the pan. Cook until the meatballs and golden brown and cooked through, 8 to 10 minutes, turning them as necessary. Transfer the cooked meatballs to a plate.

6 Divide the tabbouleh among the serving bowls, top each portion with some of the meatballs and sauce, and serve.

cauliflower tabbouleh & chicken meatballs,
see page 160

yield: 4 servings / active time: 20 minutes / total time: 30 minutes

keema curry

Keema curry is a popular dish from India that leans on a dynamic blend of herbs and spices that takes your meal on an adventurous ride. I like to serve this with rice or naan. Dig in and get ready to be transported to another part of the world!

1 cup rice

1 tablespoon extra-virgin olive oil

3 garlic cloves, minced garlic

1 tablespoon grated fresh ginger

1 large onion, chopped

1 lb. ground beef

1 teaspoon garam masala

1 tablespoon coriander

2 tablespoons tomato paste

1 teaspoon turmeric

1 teaspoon cumin

1 teaspoon Kashmiri chili powder

1 teaspoon kosher salt

1 cup water

Fresh cilantro, chopped, for garnish

Naan, for serving (optional)

Quick Pickled Salad (see page 241), for serving

1   Cook the rice according to the instructions on the package. Fluff it, cover it, and set the rice aside.

2   Place the olive oil in a large skillet and warm it over medium heat. Add the garlic and ginger and cook for 1 minute. Add the onion and cook, stirring occasionally, until it starts to brown.

3   Add the beef and cook until it is browned, about 6 minutes, breaking it up with a wooden spoon.

4   Stir in the garam masala, coriander, tomato paste, turmeric, cumin, chili powder, and salt and cook, stirring frequently, for 2 minutes.

5   Add the water and stir to incorporate. Cover the pan and cook until the beef is cooked through, about 8 minutes.

6   Divide the rice among the serving bowls and top each portion with some of the curry. Garnish with cilantro and serve with naan (if desired) and Quick Pickled Salad.

yield: 4 servings / active time: 15 minutes / total time: 25 minutes

salmon over cauliflower rice

Cauliflower's incredible versatility is a godsend for when you need to get a quick dinner on the table but are also looking to cut down on starchy carbs.

3 wild salmon fillets

Salt, to taste

3 tablespoons Dijon mustard

1½ teaspoons smoked paprika

2 tablespoons brown sugar

1 teaspoon red pepper flakes

1 tablespoon avocado oil

2 cups cauliflower rice

1 cup shelled, cooked edamame

1 cup chopped scallions

Sesame seeds, for garnish

Pickled Vegetables (see page 240), for serving

1 Preheat an air fryer to 400°F. Season the salmon with salt and spread 1 tablespoon of mustard over each fillet. Combine the paprika, brown sugar, and red pepper and then sprinkle the mixture over the salmon.

2 Place the salmon in the air fryer and cook until it is cooked through, about 10 to 12 minutes.

3 Place the avocado oil in a large skillet and warm it over medium heat. Add the cauliflower rice, season with salt, and cook, stirring occasionally, until it is tender and lightly golden brown, about 10 minutes.

4 Remove the salmon from the air fryer and chop it.

5 Divide the cauliflower rice among the serving bowls and top each portion with some of the salmon, edamame, and scallions. Garnish with sesame seeds and serve with Pickled Vegetables.

mediterranean chicken with salad & fries

A sumptuous bowl featuring plenty of veggies to keep everything in balance.

1 cup yogurt

2 tablespoons extra-virgin olive oil

½ teaspoon kosher salt

Juice of ½ lemon

1 teaspoon paprika

3 garlic cloves, minced

1 teaspoon red pepper flakes

½ teaspoon dried oregano

½ teaspoon dried parsley

1 lb. chicken thighs

1 cup chopped lettuce

1 cucumber, sliced thin

Flesh of 1 large avocado, diced

Pickled Red Onion (see page 228), for garnish

Feta cheese, crumbled, for garnish

Fresh parsley, chopped, for garnish

Tzatziki (see page 249), for serving

Pita bread, for serving

French fries, for serving

1   Place the yogurt, olive oil, salt, lemon juice, paprika, garlic, red pepper flakes, oregano, and dried parsley in a bowl and stir to combine. Add the chicken, stir to coat, and let it marinate in the refrigerator for 30 minutes.

2   Preheat the oven to 425°F. Place the chicken on a baking sheet in an even layer, place it in the oven, and roast until it is cooked through, about 15 minutes, stirring it halfway through.

3   Set the oven's broiler to high and broil the chicken until it just starts to char, about 2 minutes. Remove the chicken from the oven. Divide the lettuce among the serving bowls and top each portion with some of the chicken, cucumber, and avocado. Garnish with pickled onion, feta, and fresh parsley and serve with Tzatziki, pita bread, and French fries.

mediterranean chicken with salad & fries,
see page 167

yield: 4 servings / active time: 15 minutes / total time: 1 hour

chicken noodle soup

When you're feeling a little under the weather, or just want to make sure you give the ol' immune system a little boost, this soup is a tremendous place to turn.

2 tablespoons extra-virgin olive oil

2 bay leaves

1 tablespoon minced fresh ginger

3 garlic cloves, minced

12 cups water

2 lbs. chicken drumsticks

3 carrots, peeled and chopped (1-inch chunks)

3 celery stalks, chopped (1-inch chunks)

1 yellow onion, chopped

1 teaspoon turmeric

Salt and pepper, to taste

1½ cups wide egg noodles

Fresh parsley, chopped, for garnish

Lemon wedges, for serving

1   Place the olive oil in a large pot and warm it over medium heat. Add the bay leaves, ginger, and garlic and cook for 1 minute. Add the water and bring to a boil.

2   Add the chicken, carrots, celery, onion, and turmeric, season with salt and pepper, and reduce the heat so that the soup simmers. Cook until the chicken is tender, 30 to 35 minutes, stirring occasionally.

3   Add the egg noodles and cook until they are al dente, about 10 minutes.

4   Remove the soup from heat and let it sit for a few minutes. Remove the chicken and shred the meat with two forks.

5   Ladle the soup into warmed bowls and top each portion with some of the shredded chicken. Garnish with parsley and serve with lemon wedges.

chicken piccata

This is one of my favorite meals that my mother made when I was growing up. Though I could be a tough critic and gave her a hard time for some of the meals (Sorry, Mom!), this one was always devoured in a matter of minutes.

For the Bowls

1 lb. boneless, skinless chicken breasts, butterflied

Salt and pepper, to taste

¼ cup all-purpose flour

2 tablespoons unsalted butter

2 tablespoons extra-virgin olive oil

½ lb. pasta

For the Sauce

2 tablespoons unsalted butter

1 cup Chicken Stock (see page 227)

⅓ cup dry white wine

2 tablespoons capers in brine, drained

Juice of ½ lemon

Fresh parsley, chopped, for garnish

1   Bring water to a boil in a large saucepan.

2   To begin preparations for the bowls, season the chicken with salt and pepper. Place the flour in a shallow bowl and dredge the chicken in it until it is lightly coated, shaking off any excess.

3   Place 1 tablespoon of butter and 1 tablespoon of olive oil in a large skillet and warm the mixture over medium heat. Working in batches to avoid crowding the pan, add half of the chicken and cook until it is browned on both sides and cooked through, 6 to 8 minutes, turning it over once.

4   Remove the chicken from the pan and repeat Step 2 with the remaining butter, olive oil, and chicken.

5   Add salt and pasta to the boiling water and cook until the pasta is al dente, 8 to 10 minutes. Drain the pasta and set it aside.

6   To prepare the sauce, add the lemon juice, stock, and capers to the skillet and bring to a boil, scraping up any browned bits from the bottom of the pan. Whisk the butter into the sauce and then add the white wine.

7   Add the chicken to the pan and turn to coat it with the sauce.

8   Divide the pasta among the serving bowls and top each portion with some of the chicken and sauce. Garnish with parsley and serve.

yield: 4 servings / active time: 20 minutes / total time: 20 minutes

blackened shrimp with mango salsa

A great refreshing bowl that takes me to seaside memories—blues skies and sunshine. I can close my eyes and go back to some of my favorite places on a summer day in my backyard. A beautiful medley of flavors and colors you will not forget!

1 cup rice

1½ lb. large shrimp, shells removed, deveined

1 tablespoon paprika

1 tablespoon chili powder

1 teaspoon red pepper flakes

1 tablespoon garlic powder

1 teaspoon kosher salt

2 tablespoons extra-virgin olive oil

Cilantro Dressing (see page 237)

Mango Salsa (see page 238)

1   Cook the rice according to the directions on the package. Fluff it, cover it, and set the rice aside.

2   Pat the shrimp dry. Place the paprika, chili powder, red pepper flakes, garlic powder, and salt in a bowl and stir to combine. Add the shrimp and toss to coat.

3   Place the olive oil in a large skillet and warm it over medium heat. Add the shrimp and cook until it is cooked through, 2 to 4 minutes, turning it over halfway through.

4   Divide the rice among the serving bowls, top each portion with some of the shrimp, dressing, and salsa, and serve.

blackened shrimp with mango salsa,
see page 173

chicken biryani

This one takes some time. But man is it worth it! This chicken biryani is aromatic, has layers of flavorful rice, whole spices, caramelized onions, and succulent pieces of chicken. It is perfect for a special meal during the holiday season.

½ cup basmati rice

1½ lbs. boneless, skinless chicken thighs, cut and clean

½ cup yogurt

Salt, to taste

1 teaspoon fresh lemon juice

¼ cup canola oil

Seeds of 3 green cardamom pods

Seeds of 2 black cardamom pods

2 bay leaves

1 to 2 cinnamon sticks

3 dried red chile peppers, stemmed, seeded, and torn

2 large onions, sliced thin

1 tablespoon ginger paste

2 tablespoons garlic paste

3 tomatoes, chopped

1 teaspoon cumin

2 teaspoons coriander

2 teaspoons Kashmiri chili powder

2 teaspoons saffron threads

¼ cup warm milk

1 teaspoon garam masala

1 teaspoon finely chopped fresh cilantro

1 teaspoon finely chopped fresh mint

Crispy Onions (see page 233)

Kachumber salad (see page 134), for serving

Greek yogurt, for serving (optional)

1. Cook the rice according to the directions on the package, taking care not to over-cook it. Fluff the rice and set it aside.

2. Place the chicken and yogurt in a bowl, add salt and the lemon juice, and stir until the chicken is coated. Let the chicken marinate in the refrigerator.

3. Place the canola oil in a Dutch oven and warm it over medium heat. Add the carda-mom, bay leaves, cinnamon sticks, and chiles and stir-fry for 30 seconds.

4. Add the onions and cook, stirring occasionally, until they are tender and golden brown. Add the ginger and garlic and cook, stirring frequently, for 2 minutes.

5. Add the tomatoes and cook for 5 minutes, mashing them with a wooden spoon as they cook.

6. Stir in the cumin, coriander, and chili powder, season with salt, and then add the chicken. Cook the chicken until it is golden brown, about 5 minutes, reduce the heat, and cook until it is cooked through, about 20 minutes.

7. While the chicken is cooking, place the saffron and milk in a bowl and steep for 10 minutes. Drain the saffron, set it aside, and reserve the milk.

8. Remove the pot from heat. Cover the chicken with half of the rice, garam masala, saffron, reserved milk, cilantro, mint, and Crispy Onions. Top with the remaining rice and sprinkle the rest of the garam masala, saffron, reserved milk, cilantro, mint, and Crispy Onions on top.

9. Cover the pot and place it over the lowest possible heat. Cook for 5 minutes, turn off the heat, and let the biryani rest for 10 minutes.

10. Divide the biryani among the serving bowls and serve with kachumber salad and yogurt (if desired).

chicken biryani,
see page 176

yield: 4 servings / active time: 10 minutes / total time: 10 minutes

shrimp scampi

On days you want something simple and satisfying, cook this delicious recipe. And if you're looking for something slightly more substantial, prepare some pasta—orzo is a great option—to go alongside.

2 tablespoons unsalted butter

1 lb. shrimp, shells removed, deveined

3 garlic cloves, minced

½ teaspoon red pepper flakes

¼ cup white wine

Juice of 1 lemon

½ teaspoon kosher salt

¼ cup chopped fresh parsley, plus more for garnish

1 Place the butter in a large skillet and melt it over medium heat. Add the shrimp, garlic, and red pepper flakes and cook until the shrimp turns pink, about 3 minutes, stirring occasionally.

2 Reduce the heat to medium-low, add the wine, lemon juice, salt, and parsley and cook until the shrimp is cooked through.

3 Divide the shrimp among the serving bowls, garnish with additional parsley, and serve.

chicken khao soi

This Laotian-Burmese dish requires just a handful of ingredients, but it is comfort food at its finest.

½ lb. rice or ramen noodles

2 tablespoons avocado oil

Khao Soi Paste (see page 248)

1 lb. boneless, skinless chicken thighs chopped

1 (14 oz.) can of coconut milk

1 cup water

1 cup Crispy Onions (see page 233)

1 red onion, sliced thin

1 cup crushed peanuts

Fresh cilantro, chopped, for garnish

Chili Oil (see page 247), for garnish

Lime wedges, for serving

1 Cook the noodles according to the directions on the package and then set them aside.

2 Place the avocado oil in a medium saucepan and warm it over medium heat. Add the paste and cook, stirring frequently, for 5 minutes.

3 Add the chicken and stir to coat. Cook until the chicken is just about cooked through, about 10 minutes.

4 Add the coconut milk and water and bring to a simmer. Cook, stirring occasionally, until the sauce has thickened slightly, about 5 minutes.

5 Divide the noodles among the serving bowls and top each portion with some of the chicken, Crispy Onions, red onion, and peanuts. Garnish with cilantro and Chili Oil and serve with lime wedges.

chicken khao soi,
see page 181

chicken korma

Pair this rich, flavorful dish with a pot of cumin-spiked rice and dinner will become an occasion to remember.

2 teaspoons Kashmiri chili powder

1 teaspoon cumin

1½ teaspoons coriander

Juice of ½ lemon

1 tablespoon minced fresh ginger

3 garlic cloves, minced

1½ lbs. boneless, skinless chicken thighs, chopped

3 tablespoons avocado oil

2 large onions, diced

½ cup cashews, plus more for garnish

2 small bay leaves

Seeds of 5 green cardamom pods

6 whole peppercorns

1 cinnamon stick

1 cup yogurt

1 Place the chili powder, cumin, coriander, lemon juice, ginger, and garlic in a large bowl and stir to combine. Add the chicken, stir to coat, and marinate it in the refrigerator for 30 minutes.

2 Place 2 tablespoons of avocado oil in a Dutch oven and warm it over medium heat. Add the onions and cook, stirring occasionally, until they are a deep golden brown, 12 to 15 minutes.

3 Remove the onions from the pan, place them in a blender, and puree.

4 Using a mortar and pestle, grind the cashews into a paste, adding water as needed.

5 Place the remaining avocado oil in the Dutch oven and warm it over medium-high heat. Add the bay leaves, cardamom pods, peppercorns, and cinnamon stick and toast them for 1 minute. Add the chicken and cook until it is browned all over, 6 to 8 minutes, stirring as necessary.

6 Stir in the onion puree and cashew paste and cook for 2 minutes. Add the yogurt and cook, stirring occasionally, until the fat separates and rises to the top, about 6 minutes.

7 Divide the korma among the serving bowls, garnish with additional cashews, and serve.

lamb meatballs over salad greens

An admission: while testing this recipe, I devoured it in minutes. My guess is you will do the same, as the lamb and the blend of spices results in the most succulent meatballs.

1 lb. ground lamb

1 large onion, grated

1 teaspoon kosher salt

3 garlic cloves, minced

1 teaspoon cumin

1 teaspoon cayenne pepper

½ teaspoon cinnamon

½ cup bread crumbs

1 egg

⅓ cup chopped fresh cilantro

2 tablespoons extra-virgin olive oil

4 cups salad greens

Pickled Vegetables (see page 240)

Green Sauce (see page 235)

Fresh mint, for garnish

Pita bread or naan, for serving

1 Place the lamb, onion, salt, garlic, cumin, cayenne, cinnamon, bread crumbs, egg, and cilantro in a large bowl and work the mixture with your hands until well combined. Form heaping tablespoons of the mixture into balls and place them on a plate.

2 Place the olive oil in a large skillet and warm it over medium heat. Working in batches if necessary to avoid crowding the pan, add the meatballs and cook until they are browned all over and cooked through, 10 to 12 minutes, turning them as necessary.

3 Divide the greens among the serving bowls and top each portion with some of the meatballs, Pickled Vegetables, and sauce. Garnish with mint and serve with pitas.

yield: 4 servings / active time: 20 minutes / total time: 30 minutes

spicy sausage pasta

These bowls have been one of my go-tos since college, as they are easy to whip up and a godsend when I'm blanking on an answer to the age-old question: What's for dinner?

2 tablespoons extra-virgin olive oil

6 garlic cloves, minced

1 onion, finely diced

¾ lb. chicken sausage, chopped

Salt, to taste

10 oz. rigatoni

2 cups Marinara Sauce (see page 230)

1 teaspoon sugar

1 tablespoon red pepper flakes

3 cups spinach

Parmesan cheese, grated, for garnish

Fresh basil, for garnish

1. Bring water to a boil in a large saucepan. Place the olive oil in a medium saucepan and warm it over medium heat. Add the garlic and cook for 2 minutes.

2. Add the onion and cook, stirring occasionally, until it is translucent, about 3 minutes. Add the sausage and cook until it has browned, about 5 minutes, stirring occasionally.

3. Add salt and the pasta to the boiling water and cook until the pasta is al dente. Reserve ⅓ cup pasta water, drain the pasta, and set it aside.

4. Add the sauce, sugar, and red pepper flakes to the medium saucepan, bring to a simmer, and cook for 5 minutes. Add the spinach and cook until it has wilted, 2 to 3 minutes.

5. Add the pasta to the sauce and toss to combine, adding the reserved pasta water as needed to reach the desired consistency.

6. Divide the pasta among the serving bowls, garnish with Parmesan and basil, and serve.

chicken stew

If you have a bit more time to spare, consider roasting the mushrooms in the oven first, as it will deepen their flavor and improve the overall dish.

1 cup rice

1 tablespoon avocado oil

5 whole cloves

1 cinnamon stick

1 large onion, diced

5 garlic cloves, minced

1 lb. boneless, skinless chicken thighs, cut into thick strips

1 teaspoon kosher salt

1 teaspoon black pepper

1 (14 oz.) can of coconut milk

3 cups Chicken Stock (see page 227)

½ lb. mushrooms, sliced

Fresh parsley, chopped, for garnish

Lemon wedges, for serving

1 Cook the rice according to the directions on the package. Fluff it, cover it, and set it aside.

2 Place the avocado oil in a Dutch oven and warm it over medium heat. Add the cloves and cinnamon stick and cook for 1 minute.

3 Add the onion and cook, stirring occasionally, until it has softened, about 5 minutes. Add the garlic and cook until the onion starts to brown, about 3 minutes.

4 Add the chicken, salt, and pepper and cook until the chicken starts to brown, about 5 minutes.

5 Add the coconut milk and stock and bring to a simmer. Cook until the chicken is cooked through, about 12 minutes.

6 Add the mushrooms and cook, stirring occasionally, until the stew thickens slightly and the flavors have started to come together, about 5 minutes.

7 Divide the rice among the serving bowls and ladle the stew over each portion. Garnish with parsley and serve with lemon wedges.

yield: 4 servings / active time: 20 minutes / total time: 1 hour

chili

The first time I tried chili was at my aunt's home in Germany, and it was not until I moved to New York City—and had to find some way to survive the frigid winters— that I began experimenting with it on my own. As you can guess from that origin, this one is coming in hot. Use whichever mushroom seasoning you prefer; I use the one from Trader Joe's.

1 tablespoon extra-virgin olive oil

3 garlic cloves, minced

1 large yellow onion, chopped

1 lb. ground beef

1 teaspoon mushroom seasoning

½ teaspoon kosher salt

1 teaspoon red pepper flakes

1 teaspoon cumin

2 cups water

1 (28 oz.) can of crushed tomatoes

2 (14 oz.) cans of kidney beans, drained

2 tablespoons brown sugar

1 cup shredded cheddar cheese

1 red onion, chopped

Fresh cilantro, chopped, for garnish

Corn chips, for serving

Sour cream, for serving

1   Place the olive oil in a medium saucepan and warm it over medium heat. Add the garlic and cook for 1 minute. Add the yellow onion and cook, stirring occasionally, until it is translucent, about 3 minutes.

2   Add the beef, mushroom seasoning, salt, red pepper flakes, and cumin and cook until the beef has browned, about 6 minutes, breaking it up with a wooden spoon.

3   Add the water, tomatoes, kidney beans, and brown sugar and stir until well combined. Bring the chili to a boil, reduce the heat so that it simmers, and cook until it starts to thicken, about 35 minutes.

4   Ladle the chili into warmed bowls and top each portion with some of the cheddar cheese and red onion. Garnish with cilantro and serve with corn chips and sour cream.

snacks
& sides

As a bowl is capable of bringing together so many variables, it's easy to lose sight of snacks and side dishes when planning the weekly menu. But there will inevitably be a moment where you need to fight off an impending bout of hanger, or need one more dish to round out the table. These recipes are made for such moments, capable of coming together quickly and keeping everything in balance.

yield: 2 to 4 servings / active time: 15 minutes / total time: 35 minutes

chana chaat

Chaat is a family of savory snacks that originated in India and are typically served as an hors d'oeuvre or on the roadside tracks. Chana Chaat is a spiced tangy chickpea salad that features sev, which is small pieces of crunchy noodles made from chickpea flour, generously seasoned with spices.

1 large russet potato, rinsed well and diced

1 cup yogurt

Pinch of sugar

½ teaspoon kosher salt

½ teaspoon roasted cumin

1 teaspoon Kashmiri chili powder

1 teaspoon minced fresh ginger

1 (14 oz.) can of chickpeas, drained

1 small onion, chopped

2 tablespoons Mint Chutney (see page 247)

⅓ cup tamarind chutney

1 cup sev

1 cup pomegranate arils

Fresh cilantro, chopped, for garnish

1   Bring water to a boil in a medium saucepan. Add the potato and cook until it is tender, about 15 minutes. Drain and set the potato aside.

2   Place the yogurt, sugar, salt, cumin, chili powder, and ginger in a bowl and stir until well combined.

3   Divide the yogurt mixture among the serving bowls and top each portion with some of the chickpeas, boiled potatoes, onion, Mint Chutney, tamarind chutney, sev, and pomegranate. Garnish with cilantro and serve.

lemon rice

A simple bowl guaranteed to brighten your day and mood, this flavorful side is a perfect way to use up a day-old rice.

2 tablespoons avocado oil

2 dried red chile peppers, stemmed, seeded, and minced

10 to 12 dried curry leaves

1 tablespoon chana dal

3 tablespoons raw peanuts

Pinch of hing powder (asafoetida)

½ teaspoon turmeric

Salt, to taste

2 cups leftover rice

Juice of ½ lemon

Roasted cashews, for garnish

1 Place the avocado oil in a large skillet and warm it over medium heat. Add the chiles, curry leaves, chana dal, and peanuts and stir-fry until the mixture is aromatic, 1 to 2 minutes.

2 Stir in the hing powder and turmeric and season with salt. Add the rice and lemon juice and stir until well combined.

3 Cook until the rice is warmed through. Taste and adjust the seasoning as necessary. Divide the rice among the serving bowls, garnish with cashews, and serve.

yield: 4 servings / active time: 10 minutes / total time: 25 minutes

aloo chaat

Let me introduce you to some street style snacks from the Indian subcontinent. The textures and flavors in this one are not for the faint of the heart, but I promise you, it is a gastronomic roller coaster you want to take!

2 large russet potatoes

2 tablespoons avocado oil

1 teaspoon roasted cumin

½ teaspoon Kashmiri chili powder

1 teaspoon minced fresh ginger

1 teaspoon chaat masala

2 tablespoons tamarind chutney

1 tablespoon Mint Chutney (see page 247)

1 tablespoon fresh lemon juice

2 tablespoons chopped fresh cilantro

½ cup pomegranate arils, for garnish

1 Preheat an air fryer to 350°F. Rinse the potatoes and scrub them. Cut the potatoes into large chunks and place them in the air fryer. Brush them with the avocado oil and cook until they are crispy and tender, about 16 minutes, turning them over halfway through.

2 Remove the potatoes from the air fryer and place them in a large bowl. Add the remaining ingredients, except for the pomegranate arils, and stir to combine.

3 Divide the aloo chaat between the serving bowls, garnish with the pomegranate arils, and serve.

aloo chaat,
see page 199

yield: 4 servings / active time: 5 minutes / total time: 25 minutes

crunchy chickpeas

These snack bowls are inspired by a beloved street food in India—chana chor garam. To get a more authentic version, incorporate red onion, cucumber, tomato, chaat masala, and lemon juice after cooking the chickpeas.

1 (14 oz.) can of chickpeas, drained

1 tablespoon avocado oil

½ teaspoon cumin

½ teaspoon cayenne pepper

½ teaspoon kosher salt

1 Preheat an air fryer for 375°F. Place all of the ingredients in a mixing bowl and stir to coat.

2 Place the chickpeas in the air fryer and cook until they are crunchy and golden brown, 15 to 18 minutes.

3 Remove the chickpeas from the air fryer and serve.

spicy edamame

These are perfect for that wonderful moment when you recognize that snacks don't have to be filled with refined carbs and sugar. Protein-packed, these bowls will provide satisfaction and enough energy to help you go the extra mile.

½ lb. frozen, shelled edamame

1 teaspoon brown sugar

½ teaspoon red pepper flakes

½ teaspoon kosher salt

Juice of 1 lemon

1 Cook the edamame according to the directions on the package.

2 Let the edamame cool.

3 Place the edamame in a bowl, add the remaining ingredients, and stir to combine.

4 Divide among the serving bowls or store in the refrigerator for up to 4 days.

yield: 4 servings / active time: 5 minutes / total time: 5 minutes

high-protein nacho cheese dip

A wonderful bowl for game nights and parties alike! Packed with great flavor, it is sure to spark great conversations and create lasting memories.

2 cups cottage cheese

½ cup sour cream

1 tablespoon Mexican seasoning blend (see page 93)

¾ cup shredded Mexican-style cheese

Crackers, for serving (optional)

Crudités, for serving (optional)

1   Place the cottage cheese, sour cream, seasoning blend, and half of the shredded cheese in a food processor and blitz until well combined, scraping down the work bowl as necessary.

2   Transfer the dip to a serving bowl and top with the remaining shredded cheese. Serve with crackers or crudités.

yield: 4 servings / active time: 5 minutes / total time: 5 minutes

raita

A good bowl of Ratia has a refreshing quality that goes a long way in complementing spicy dishes, making it a wonderful side dish for a number of the preparations in this book.

2 cups Greek yogurt

1 green chile pepper, stemmed, seeded, and chopped

4 Persian cucumbers, peeled and grated

1 garlic clove, grated

¼ teaspoon cumin

½ teaspoon kosher salt

Fresh cilantro, for garnish

1 Place all of the ingredients, except for the cilantro, in a serving bowl and stir to combine.

2 Taste and adjust the seasoning as necessary. Garnish with cilantro and divide among the serving bowls or store in the refrigerator for up to 1 day.

yield: 4 servings / active time: 10 minutes / total time: 35 minutes

bhel puri with aam papad

Two delicious Indian street foods in one bowl? Yes please! This bowl built around bhel puri, a snack mix featuring sev and puffed rice, comes from a place of love, and is certain to add some sunshine to your day.

Salt, to taste

1 potato, peeled and diced

4 cups bhel puri mix

1 small red onion, sliced thin

1 tomato, chopped

½ cup tamarind chutney

½ cup Mint Chutney (see page 247)

½ cup aam papad

½ teaspoon chaat masala

Kashmiri chili powder, to taste

Juice of 1 small lemon

½ cup sev, for garnish

Fresh cilantro, chopped, for garnish

1 Bring water to a boil in a medium saucepan. Add salt and the potato and cook until the potato is tender, about 15 minutes. Drain the potato and let it cool.

2 Place the bhel puri, potato, onion, and tomato in a bowl and gently stir to combine.

3 Add the chutneys and aam papad and gently stir to combine. You can add the amount of chutneys as per the taste you want in a bhel puri.

4 Add the chaat masala, chili powder, and lemon juice and gently stir to combine.

5 Divide the bhel puri among the serving bowls, garnish with the sev and cilantro, and serve.

bhel puri with aam papad,
see page 209

desserts

With all of this time spent in the kitchen constructing delicious bowls, it is inevitable that a craving for something sweet will arise. These sumptuous desserts are the perfect reply, as they are easy to put together and certain to satisfy.

yield: 4 servings / active time: 20 minutes / total time: 30 minutes

kheer

Kheer is a popular dessert from India, made by slow cooking rice, milk, and sugar. Eventually, these come together in a dessert that features an irresistibly subtle fragrance and a creamy texture. This version gets extra points for being vegan-friendly.

¼ cup rice

4 cups oat milk

2 teaspoons cardamom

5 tablespoons sugar

1 teaspoon saffron threads, plus more to taste

Pistachios, chopped, for garnish

1 Place the rice in a bowl, cover it with cold water, and let it soak for 30 minutes.

2 Drain the rice and rinse it under cold water until the water runs clear.

3 Place the oat milk in a medium saucepan and bring it to a boil. Reduce the heat so that the oat milk simmers and add the rice. Cook until the rice is al dente and the milk has reduced by half, about 15 minutes.

4 Stir in the cardamom, sugar, and saffron and simmer until the pudding starts to thicken, about 10 minutes. If desired, add some additional saffron.

5 Remove the pudding from heat and let it cool. Serve chilled or at room temperature, garnishing each portion with pistachios.

yield: 4 servings / active time: 30 minutes / total time: 2 hours and 45 minutes

badam kheer

This is a creamy, rich, and delicious pudding made with almonds, milk, sugar, cardamom, and saffron. This dessert tastes festive, making it a great choice for celebrations and holidays.

¾ cup almonds, plus more for garnish

4 cups whole milk

2 teaspoons ground cardamom

1 teaspoon saffron threads

¼ cup sugar

1   Cover the almonds with warm water and let them soak for 2 hours.

2   Drain the almonds, remove their skins, and grind the almonds into a paste, adding a few drops of water if necessary.

3   Place the milk in a saucepan and bring to a boil. Reduce the heat so that the milk simmers and cook for 15 minutes.

4   Stir in the almond paste and cook until the milk has reduced by half.

5   Stir in the remaining ingredients and simmer until the pudding starts to thicken, about 10 minutes.

6   Transfer the pudding to a bowl and let it cool. Serve at room temperature or chilled, and garnish each portion with additional almonds.

badam kheer,
see page 215

yield: 4 servings / active time: 10 minutes / total time: 30 minutes

mango sago

This is a chilled mango pudding that originated in Hong Kong and is now popular throughout East and Southeast Asian countries. It is an easy-to-make, refreshing dessert that will help you keep cool for the summer.

¾ cup tapioca pearls

Flesh of 3 large mangoes, chopped, plus more for garnish

1 (14 oz.) can of coconut milk

½ cup condensed milk

1   Bring 4 cups of water to a boil in a medium saucepan. Add the tapioca pearls and cook until they are completely transparent, about 20 minutes.

2   Place the mangoes and coconut milk in a blender and puree until smooth.

3   Transfer the mixture to a bowl, stir in the condensed milk, and chill the mixture in the refrigerator.

4   Drain the tapioca and stir it into the mango mixture.

5   Divide the mango sago among the serving bowls, garnish each portion with additional mango, and serve.

peanut butter ice cream

OK, so it's not technically ice cream! But it makes you feel like you had it is and it tastes amazing. Add in that it's actually healthy and you've got a winning dessert.

3 large peeled bananas, frozen

¼ cup unsweetened cocoa powder

2 tablespoons peanut butter

⅓ cup chopped dark chocolate

⅓ cup milk

Roasted peanuts, chopped, for garnish

1   Place the milk, cocoa powder, bananas, and peanut butter in a food processor and blitz until the mixture is very smooth.

2   Add the chocolate and blitz until incorporated.

3   Transfer the mixture to a 9 x 5–inch loaf pan and cover it with plastic wrap, placing it directly on the surface of the ice cream.

4   Freeze the ice cream until it is solid, 2 to 4 hours.

5   Scoop the ice cream into the serving bowls, garnish each portion with peanuts, and serve.

yield: 4 servings / active time: 20 minutes / total time: 2 hours and 30 minutes

no-bake lime cheesecakes

I made these for a party once, and they were a big hit! I'm betting you'll find similar success. Best of all, it's a great make-ahead dessert.

6 oz. graham crackers

2 tablespoons unsalted butter, melted

¼ cup cream cheese

⅓ cup confectioners' sugar

1 teaspoon pure vanilla extract

3 tablespoons fresh lemon juice

Zest of 1 lemon, plus more for garnish

2 cups Cool Whip, thawed

1 Place the graham crackers in a food processor and blitz until they are fine crumbs. Add the butter and blitz to combine.

2 Split the graham cracker mixture between bowls or ramekins, press down firmly on it with the back of a spoon, and then chill the crusts in the freezer for 10 minutes.

3 Place the cream cheese in the work bowl of a stand mixer fitted with the paddle attachment and beat for 30 seconds. Add the confectioners' sugar, vanilla, lemon juice, and lemon zest and beat until well combined.

4 Working in two increments, add the Cool Whip and fold to incorporate it.

5 Using a rubber spatula, transfer the filling to a piping bag fitted with a regular tip. You can also place it in a resealable plastic bag and cut a 1-inch hole in one of the corners.

6 Pipe the filling over the crusts and chill the cheese-cakes in the refrigerator for 2 hours.

7 Garnish with additional lemon zest and serve.

yield: 4 servings / active time: 20 minutes / total time: 24 hours

easy mango ice cream

Level up your dessert game with this divine homemade ice cream, which I've loved since childhood. If you prefer to use frozen mango puree instead of fresh mangoes, substitute 2 cups.

4 cups whole milk

⅓ cup sugar

Flesh of 3 mangoes, chopped

1 cup heavy cream

1 Place the milk in a medium saucepan and bring to a boil, stirring continually. Cook until the milk has reduced by half, remove the pan from heat, and let it cool slightly.

2 Add the sugar and stir to dissolve. Let the milk mixture cool completely.

3 Place the mangoes in a blender and puree until smooth.

4 Add the cream and mango puree to the milk mixture and stir until well combined. Pour the mixture into a glass container and cover it with plastic wrap, placing it directly on the surface.

5 Freeze the ice cream overnight. To serve, scoop into bowls.

appendix

yield: 16 cups / active time: 1 hour / total time: 10 hours

chicken stock

4 lbs. leftover chicken bones

32 cups cold water

¼ cup white wine

1 onion, chopped

1 celery stalk, chopped

1 carrot, chopped

2 bay leaves

10 sprigs of fresh parsley

10 sprigs of fresh thyme

1 teaspoon black peppercorns

Salt, to taste

1   Preheat the oven to 400°F. Place the chicken bones on a baking sheet, place them in the oven, and roast them until they are caramelized, about 1 hour.

2   Remove the chicken bones from the oven and place them in a stockpot. Cover them with the water and bring to a boil, skimming to remove any impurities that rise to the surface.

3   Deglaze the baking sheet with the white wine, scraping up any browned bits from the bottom. Stir the liquid into the stock, add the remaining ingredients, and reduce the heat so that the stock simmers. Simmer the stock until it has reduced by three-quarters and the flavor is to your liking, about 6 hours, skimming the surface as needed.

4   Strain the stock and either use immediately or let it cool completely and store it in the refrigerator.

yield: 3 cups / active time: 10 minutes / total time: 25 minutes

arrabbiata sauce

2 tablespoons extra-virgin olive oil

3 garlic cloves, crushed

2 dried chile peppers, stemmed, seeded, and chopped

1 (28 oz.) can of peeled whole San Marzano tomatoes, with their liquid

Handful of fresh parsley, chopped

Salt and pepper, to taste

1 Warm a large skillet over low heat for 1 to 2 minutes. Add the olive oil, garlic, and chiles, raise the heat to medium-low, and cook until the garlic begins to brown, about 1 minute.

2 Remove the garlic and as much of the chiles as possible and add the tomatoes, crushing them with your hands as you add them to the pan. Add the liquid from the can, raise the heat to medium-high, and bring the sauce to a boil. Reduce the heat to medium-low and cook, stirring occasionally, until the sauce has thickened, about 20 minutes.

3 Stir in the parsley, season the sauce with salt and pepper, and use immediately or store in the refrigerator.

---

yield: 2 cups / active time: 10 minutes / total time: 2 hours

pickled red onion

½ cup apple cider vinegar

½ cup water

2 tablespoons kosher salt

2 tablespoons sugar

1 red onion, sliced thin

1 Place the vinegar, water, salt, and sugar in a saucepan and bring to a boil, stirring to dissolve the salt and sugar.

2 Place the onion in a bowl, pour the brine over it, and let it cool completely.

3 Transfer the onion and brine to a mason jar and store it in the refrigerator.

yield: 1 cup / active time: 20 minutes / total time: 1 hour

harissa sauce

1 head of garlic, halved at the equator

2 tablespoons extra-virgin olive oil

2 bell peppers

2 tablespoons coriander seeds

6 chiles de árbol

3 pasilla chile peppers

2 shallots, halved

2 teaspoons kosher salt

1   Preheat the oven to 400°F. Place the garlic in a piece of aluminum foil, drizzle half of the olive oil over it, and seal the foil closed.

2   Place the garlic on a baking sheet with the bell peppers and place it in the oven. Roast until the garlic is very tender and the peppers are charred all over. Remove them from the oven and let them cool.

3   While the garlic and peppers are cooling, place the coriander seeds in a dry skillet and toast them over medium heat, shaking the pan frequently. Transfer the coriander seeds to a blender along with the remaining ingredients, including the remaining olive oil.

4   Squeeze the roasted garlic cloves into the blender. Remove the skin, seeds, and stems from the roasted peppers and place the flesh in the blender.

5   Puree until the harissa paste has the desired texture and use immediately or store it in the refrigerator.

marinara sauce

4 lbs. tomatoes, peeled, seeded, and chopped

1 yellow onion, sliced

15 garlic cloves, crushed

2 teaspoons fresh thyme

2 teaspoons fresh oregano

2 tablespoons extra-virgin olive oil

1½ tablespoons kosher salt, plus more to taste

1 teaspoon black pepper, plus more to taste

2 tablespoons finely chopped fresh basil

1 tablespoon finely chopped fresh parsley

1 Place all of the ingredients, except for the basil and parsley, in a large saucepan and cook, stirring constantly, over medium heat until the tomatoes begin to collapse, about 10 minutes.

2 Reduce the heat to low and cook, stirring occasionally, for about 1½ hours, or until the flavor is to your liking.

3 Stir in the basil and parsley and season the sauce to taste. The sauce will be chunky. If you prefer a smoother texture, transfer the sauce to a food processor and blitz before serving it over pasta.

yield: 6 cups / active time: 20 minutes / total time: 3 hours

vegetable stock

2 tablespoons extra-virgin olive oil

2 large leeks, trimmed and rinsed well

2 large carrots, peeled and sliced

2 celery stalks, sliced

2 large yellow onions, sliced

3 garlic cloves, unpeeled but smashed

2 sprigs of fresh parsley

2 sprigs of fresh thyme

1 bay leaf

8 cups water

½ teaspoon black peppercorns

Salt, to taste

1 Place the olive oil and vegetables in a large stockpot and cook over low heat until the liquid they release has evaporated. This will allow the flavor of the vegetables to become concentrated.

2 Add the garlic, parsley, thyme, bay leaf, water, peppercorns, and salt. Raise the heat to high and bring to a boil. Reduce the heat so that the stock simmers and cook for 2 hours, while skimming to remove any impurities that float to the surface.

3 Strain through a fine-mesh sieve, let the stock cool slightly, and place in the refrigerator, uncovered, to chill. Remove the fat layer and cover the stock. The stock will keep in the refrigerator for 3 to 5 days, and in the freezer for up to 3 months.

yield: 8 servings / active time: 10 minutes / total time: 2 days

labneh

4 cups full-fat Greek yogurt

½ teaspoon fine sea salt

1 tablespoon extra-virgin olive oil

2 teaspoons za'atar

1 Place the yogurt in a large bowl and season it with the salt; the salt helps pull out excess whey, giving you a creamier, thicker labneh.

2 Place a fine-mesh strainer on top of a medium-sized bowl. Line the strainer with cheesecloth or a linen towel, letting a few inches hang over the side of the strainer. Spoon the seasoned yogurt into the cheesecloth and gently wrap the sides over the top of the yogurt, protecting it from being exposed to air in the refrigerator.

3 Store everything in the refrigerator for 24 to 48 hours, discarding the whey halfway through if the bowl beneath the strainer becomes too full.

4 Remove the labneh from the cheesecloth and store it in an airtight container.

5 To serve, drizzle the olive oil over the labneh and sprinkle the za'atar on top.

yield: 4 servings / active time: 30 minutes / total time: 1 hour

crispy onions

1 small onion, sliced thin

1 cup buttermilk

2 cups canola oil

½ cup all-purpose flour

½ cup cornstarch

Salt and pepper, to taste

1 Place the onion and buttermilk in a bowl and soak for 30 minutes.

2 Place the canola oil in a Dutch oven and warm it to 375°F.

3 Combine the flour and cornstarch in a shallow bowl. Dredge the onion in the mixture until it is completely coated.

4 Gently slip the onion into the hot oil one at a time and fry until crispy and golden brown.

5 Remove the fried onion from hot oil and transfer it to a paper towel–lined plate to drain. Season with salt and pepper before serving.

yield: ⅔ cup / active time: 10 minutes / total time: 20 minutes

parsley & chili oil

⅓ cup chopped fresh parsley

1 teaspoon cumin

1 teaspoon Kashmiri chili powder

1 teaspoon Aleppo pepper

3 garlic cloves, minced

½ teaspoon kosher salt

⅓ cup extra-virgin olive oil

1 Place all of the ingredients, except for the olive oil, in a heatproof bowl and stir to combine.

2 Place the olive oil in a small saucepan and warm it over medium heat. Pour the olive oil over the parsley mixture and let it cool slightly before using.

yield: ½ cup / active time: 5 minutes / total time: 5 minutes

green sauce

2 tablespoons Greek yogurt

¼ cup chopped fresh cilantro

¼ cup chopped fresh mint

1 garlic clove

¼ teaspoon kosher salt

1 jalapeño chile pepper, stemmed, seeded, and chopped (optional)

1 Place all of the ingredients in a blender and puree until smooth. Use immediately or store in the refrigerator.

cilantro sauce

Flesh of 1 avocado

1 garlic clove

¼ cup chopped fresh cilantro

Juice of ½ lemon

Splash of water

2 tablespoons chopped onion

Salt, to taste

½ jalapeño chile pepper, chopped

1 Place all of the ingredients in a blender and puree until smooth. Use immediately or store in the refrigerator.

yield: ½ cup / active time: 5 minutes / total time: 5 minutes

spicy mayo

¼ cup mayonnaise

¼ cup sriracha

1 Place the ingredients in a blender and puree until smooth. Use immediately or store in the refrigerator.

---

yield: 2 cups / active time: 5 minutes / total time: 5 minutes

cilantro dressing

⅓ cup Greek yogurt

1½ cups fresh cilantro

1 tablespoon extra-virgin olive oil

Flesh of 1 large avocado

1 garlic clove

¼ cup water

½ teaspoon kosher salt

Juice of 1 lime

1 Place all of the ingredients in a blender and puree until smooth. Use immediately or store in the refrigerator.

yield: 4 servings / active time: 5 minutes / total time: 5 minutes

mango salsa

Flesh of 1 large mango, diced

1 jalapeño chile pepper, stemmed, seeded, and minced

¼ cup chopped fresh cilantro

1 tomato, chopped

1 small red onion, finely diced

½ teaspoon kosher salt

Juice of 1 lime

1 Place the mango, jalapeño, cilantro, tomato, and onion in a small bowl and stir to combine.

2 Add the salt and lime juice and stir to incorporate. Use immediately or store in the refrigerator.

---

yield: ½ cup / active time: 5 minutes / total time: 5 minutes

sriracha sour cream

⅓ cup sour cream

3 tablespoons sriracha

1 Place the ingredients in a bowl and stir to combine. Use immediately or store in the refrigerator.

yield: ¾ cup / active time: 5 minutes / total time: 5 minutes

peanut sauce

½ cup creamy peanut butter

5 to 6 garlic cloves, grated

3 tablespoons soy sauce

1 tablespoon rice vinegar

1 teaspoon red pepper flakes

1 Place all of the ingredients in a bowl and whisk until well combined. Use immediately or store in the refrigerator.

---

yield: 8 servings / active time: 5 minutes / total time: 25 minutes

sumac onions

2 small red onions, sliced thin

2 tablespoons chopped fresh parsley

1 tablespoon sumac

½ teaspoon kosher salt

½ teaspoon sugar

Juice of ½ lemon

1 Place all of the ingredients in a bowl and stir to combine. Let the onions sit for 20 minutes before using or storing in the refrigerator.

pickled vegetables

3 cups thinly sliced vegetables (red onion, carrot, cucumber, cabbage, and beets are good options, but feel free to experiment with your favorites)

1 garlic clove, grated

⅓ cup white vinegar

½ teaspoon cayenne pepper

1 tablespoon kosher salt

1 tablespoon sugar

1 Place the vegetables and garlic in a mason jar.

2 Place the remaining ingredients in a saucepan and bring to a boil, stirring to dissolve the salt and sugar. Pour the brine into the mason jar and let the vegetables sit until they are completely cool. Use as desired or store in the refrigerator.

quick pickled salad

4 Persian cucumbers, sliced thin

1 large carrot, sliced thin

1 tablespoon rice vinegar

Pinch of sugar

Pinch of kosher salt

⅓ cup chopped fresh herbs (mint and cilantro)

1 Place all of the ingredients in a bowl and stir to combine. Let the salad sit for 20 minutes before using or storing in the refrigerator.

cilantro chutney

½ cup fresh cilantro

1 tablespoon peanuts
(optional)

½ teaspoon cumin

¼ teaspoon kosher salt

Pinch of sugar

1 garlic clove, grated

Juice of ½ lemon

1   Place all of the ingredients in a blender and puree until smooth. Use immediately or store in the refrigerator.

yield: 8 servings / active time: 5 minutes / total time: 5 minutes

spicy green chutney

½ cup fresh cilantro

½ cup fresh mint

1 tablespoon peanuts (optional)

½ teaspoon cumin

½ teaspoon Kashmiri chili powder

¼ teaspoon kosher salt

Pinch of sugar

1 garlic clove, grated

Juice of ½ lemon

1 Place all of the ingredients in a blender and puree until smooth. Use immediately or store in the refrigerator.

smashed cucumber salad

4 to 6 Persian cucumbers, chopped

½ teaspoon Kashmiri chili powder

½ teaspoon sugar

1 teaspoon white vinegar

1 garlic clove, grated

½ teaspoon kosher salt

1 Using the flat side of a knife, smash each cucumber.

2 Place the remaining ingredients in a bowl and stir until well combined. Add the cucumbers and toss to coat. Let the cucumbers marinate for 20 minutes before using or storing in the refrigerator.

yield: 2 servings / active time: 5 minutes / total time: 5 minutes

chunky monkey

1 banana, peeled and sliced

1 tablespoon peanut butter

2 tablespoons dark chocolate chips

Walnuts, crushed, to taste

1 Place all of the ingredients in a bowl and stir to combine. Use immediately.

---

yield: 2 servings / active time: 5 minutes / total time: 5 minutes

berry blast

¼ cup sliced strawberries

¼ cup sliced raspberries

1 tablespoon maple syrup

1 tablespoon chia seeds

Sliced almonds, to taste

1 Place all of the ingredients in a bowl and stir to combine. Use immediately.

yield: 2 servings / active time: 5 minutes / total time: 5 minutes

cinnamon apple

½ cup diced apple

1 teaspoon brown sugar
or maple syrup

Pinch of cinnamon

Sliced almonds, to taste

1 tablespoon pumpkin
seeds

1 Place all of the ingredients in a bowl and stir to combine. Use immediately.

---

yield: 4 servings / active time: 5 minutes / total time: 5 minutes

pico de gallo

1 small white onion,
finely diced

2 to 3 tomatoes,
finely diced

1 jalapeño chile pepper,
stemmed, seeded, and
finely diced

Juice of 1 lime

½ teaspoon kosher salt

1 Place all of the ingredients in a bowl and gently stir to combine. Use immediately or store in the refrigerator.

yield: 1 cup / active time: 10 minutes / total time: 40 minutes

chili oil

1 teaspoon cayenne pepper

1 tablespoon red pepper flakes

5 garlic cloves, minced

1 star anise pod

½ teaspoon kosher salt

½ teaspoon sugar

1 cup canola oil

1 Place all of the ingredients, except for the canola oil, in a heatproof bowl and stir to combine.

2 Place the canola oil in a small saucepan and warm it over medium heat. Pour the canola oil over the garlic mixture. Once everything starts to gently sizzle, give it a good stir. Let the oil cool and remove the star anise.

3 Use or store in an airtight jar for up to 1 month. If you store the oil, shake well before using.

---

yield: ½ cup servings / active time: 5 minutes / total time: 5 minutes

mint chutney

½ cup fresh mint

1 tablespoon peanuts (optional)

½ teaspoon cumin

¼ teaspoon kosher salt

Pinch of sugar

Juice of ½ lemon

1 Place all of the ingredients in a blender and puree until smooth. Use immediately or store in the refrigerator.

yield: ½ cup / active time: 5 minutes / total time: 5 minutes

khao soi paste

3 tablespoons avocado oil

1 onion, chopped

6 garlic cloves, chopped

1-inch piece of fresh ginger, chopped

1½ teaspoons Kashmiri chili powder

1 teaspoon cumin

1 teaspoon coriander

½ teaspoon turmeric

2 tablespoons besan (gram flour)

1 Place all of the ingredients in a blender and puree until smooth. Use immediately or store in the refrigerator.

---

yield: 8 servings / active time: 5 minutes / total time: 5 minutes

tzatziki

½ cup finely grated cucumber

1 cup Greek yogurt

1 garlic clove, minced

2 tablespoons chopped fresh herbs (mint, parsley, dill)

1 tablespoon extra-virgin olive oil

1 teaspoon kosher salt

1 Place all of the ingredients in a bowl and stir to combine. Use immediately or store in the refrigerator.

conversion table

WEIGHTS

1 oz. = 28 grams

2 oz. = 57 grams

4 oz. (¼ lb.) = 113 grams

8 oz. (½ lb.) = 227 grams

16 oz. (1 lb.) = 454 grams

VOLUME MEASURES

⅛ teaspoon = 0.6 ml

¼ teaspoon = 1.23 ml

½ teaspoon = 2.5 ml

1 teaspoon = 5 ml

1 tablespoon (3 teaspoons) = ½ fluid oz. = 15 ml

2 tablespoons = 1 fluid oz. = 29.5 ml

¼ cup (4 tablespoons) = 2 fluid oz. = 59 ml

⅓ cup (5⅓ tablespoons) = 2.7 fluid oz. = 80 ml

½ cup (8 tablespoons) = 4 fluid oz. = 120 ml

⅔ cup (10⅔ tablespoons) = 5.4 fluid oz. = 160 ml

¾ cup (12 tablespoons) = 6 fluid oz. = 180 ml

1 cup (16 tablespoons) = 8 fluid oz. = 240 ml

TEMPERATURE EQUIVALENTS

°F	°C	Gas Mark
225	110	¼
250	130	½
275	140	1
300	150	2
325	170	3
350	180	4
375	190	5
400	200	6
425	220	7
450	230	8
475	240	9
500	250	10

LENGTH MEASURES

¹⁄₁₆ inch = 1.6 mm

⅛ inch = 3 mm

¼ inch = 6.35 mm

½ inch = 1.25 cm

¾ inch = 2 cm

1 inch = 2.5 cm

index

acknowledgments

To my beloved family—my roots and my wings—I owe the deepest appreciation! From the tender age when my mom first handed me a spoon and patiently guided me through the basics of cooking, imparting the skills and wisdom that laid the foundation for my culinary journey, to my dad's unwavering praise that fueled my culinary dreams, and to my little brother whose adventurous spirit made every kitchen experiment a shared delight!

Marriage ushered in a new chapter, where my supportive in-laws embraced my aspirations with open arms, forever encouraging me to dream boldly. My husband, Maninder, my rock and confidant, has been my guiding star. To my son, Vir, whose innocent curiosity and profound questions remind me daily of the wonder in simple moments—you are my inspiration to strive for excellence.

This journey from conception to completion would not have been possible without the incredible team at Cider Mill Press. Your expertise, patience, and unwavering support have transformed my vision into reality.

about cider mill press book publishers

Good ideas ripen with time. From seed to harvest, Cider Mill Press brings fine reading, information, and entertainment together between the covers of its creatively crafted books. Our Cider Mill bears fruit twice a year, publishing a new crop of titles each spring and fall.

"Where Good Books Are Ready for Press"
501 Nelson Place
Nashville, Tennessee 37214

cidermillpress.com